MORE REMARKABLE RECIPES

TO MARK,
WHO INSPIRES US ALL TO BE
MORE REMARKABLE
IN OUR LIVING

MORE
reMARKable
RECIPES

FROM THE RECIPE FILE OF MRS. MARK O. HATFIELD

BY

ANTOINETTE KUZMANICH HATFIELD

CRITERION INC. / PUBLISHERS

P.O. BOX 81 · BEAVERTON, OREGON 97005

Library of Congress
Catalog Card No. 74-136295

Copyright © 1970
Antoinette Kuzmanich Hatfield
Printed in the United States of America

Table of Contents

Acknowledgments

To each of you who was willing to share a treasured recipe with me (and now my readers), a sincere "Thank You."

To my family and friends who were willing to "try something new to eat," my gratitude for being such good "tasters."

To Debbie Coe, Kim Wittwer, Raona Seavey and Marilyn Isaac, hugs and kisses for doing the mundane part of this book . . . the typing and proofing and prodding.

To my readers . . . we couldn't do it without you!

Preface

Every two years someone says, "It's time for a change," and that is exactly how some of you who have *ReMARKable Recipes* must feel. Hence, four years after my first endeavor at "cook bookery," I present for you a wanted, I hope, change for more "happy cooking."

Some of the same names appear in front of the recipes as were in *ReMARKable Recipes.* This indicates that just because one moves from Oregon to the nation's capitol, one does not lose friends, but rather adds more friends. You will note that there are some familiar "names in the news", too — Washington is full of such people. The important thing to remember is that those names belong to human beings, people who have hopes, desires, needs, and dreams just like anyone else . . . and they cook, too. Perhaps the reason so many political wives talk "recipes" is that it is pretty neutral ground, and, like love, is a universal language that most people can understand. Everyone needs to eat!

Antoinette Kuzmanich Hatfield

Newport, Oregon
May, 1970

Appetizers

We still don't serve "nibbles" but other people do, so here again is the shortest section of the second book . . .

*Mary McCluer is my cousin by adoption.
Since I call her **real** aunt and uncle my Aunt
Dorothy and Uncle Charlie, we now call each
other "cousin". Mary, like her sister Ann,
is a marvelous homemaker. Every time I
visit Aunt Dorothy and Uncle Charlie, Mary
has a new recipe for me. This is one of
several of hers which will appear in the book.*

CHEDDAR-BLUE CHEESE BALL

2 ounces blue cheese
1 cup grated cheddar cheese
1 package (8 ounces) cream cheese
2 tablespoons Worcestershire sauce
1 small onion, grated, or 1 teaspoon instant onion
½ teaspoon salt
½ cup ground or chopped pecans (or walnuts)
½ cup snipped parsley

Mix cheeses, Worcestershire sauce, onion and salt
with one-half nuts and one-half parsley. Chill
thoroughly. Shape into a ball and roll in remaining
nuts and parsley. Serve surrounded by crackers.
Makes about 3 cups of spread.

*Betty Howeisner served this dip at a summer
party. It was one of the first trips I'd had
"home to Salem" since going to Washington.
The dip was not only good, but so was the
company . . . there's nothing like seeing the
"home town folks."*

CURRIED CLAM DIP

Melt 4 tablespoons butter in pan over hot water.
Add ½ clove, crushed garlic and 1 teaspoon curry
powder, blend and cook for two minutes, then add
4 tablespoons flour and blend well. Add juice from
two 7 ½-ounce cans minced clams and cook until
thickened, then add the clams and heat. Serve in
chafing dish with toast rounds or crackers. This
makes about 30 servings, depending on how big a
serving each one takes!

There are many festivals throughout the state of Oregon. Each focuses on the product of unique natural resource of the area. The Astoria Regatta is one of the oldest and most colorful. Harry and Mary Steinbock, as the official hosts (he is the mayor), have added a dimension of warm hospitality to the "doings" during regatta weekend. One year Mark was the "Admiral" and Mary sent me this recipe for Tuna-Sturgeon Appetizers and a box of the main ingredients. Thanks, Mary!

TUNA-STURGEON APPETIZERS

1 can (6 ounces) tuna fish, drained
1 can smoked sturgeon
Mayonnaise
Juice of one lemon
1 teaspoon grated onion
Paprika
Parmesan cheese

Mix together tuna fish and sturgeon and add enough mayonnaise to moisten. Add lemon juice and the grated onion. Spread on toasted rounds of bread. Sprinkle with Parmesan cheese and paprika. Put into broiler. Watch carefully, as they burn very easily.

Beverages

So many of you have written to ask for something new and different to serve in the way of "beverages for those of us who don't drink." Any of the following will do, but the most effective and most fun is to fool your non-drinking (and drinking) friends by serving sparkling catawba juice in champagne style glasses. To give a brand name here would be out of order, but just ask your grocer. You'll have everyone checking the label to "be sure" one way or the other.

*After campaigning one fall evening . . . I
might add it was cold and raining . . . we
stopped by Betty and Ray Underwood's house
when they lived in Oswego. The minute the
door opened we could smell this delicious
cider simmering. It had the most inviting
smell . . . it tasted delicious and warmed our
cold bones as we sipped it before a roaring
fire. I asked Betty for the recipe . . . she said
it was so easy she was embarrassed . . . it is
easy, but you'll never be embarrassed to serve
this. I often have it simmering just for the
"good smell" . . . simmering seems to do
away with the "raw" cider taste.*

BETTY UNDERWOOD'S FRAGRANT CIDER

1 gallon sweet apple cider
3-4 sticks of "stick cinnamon"
Let simmer for two to three hours. Serve Hot!

CRANBERRY-APPLE JUICE PUNCH

Even before "cranapple juice" was bottled, I mixed
equal parts of apple and cranberry juice and added
equal parts of ginger ale. This is the half-sister to the
still popular apple juice punch.

Mrs. Clay Myers, wife of Oregon's Secretary of State, sent me this recipe. I had read in the paper that she had entertained for the wives of legislators at a clever educational coffee and had served this chocolate. Cheers for Elizabeth's creative entertaining and for sharing this recipe.

ELIZABETH MYERS' FRENCH CHOCOLATE

Combine ¾ cup semi-sweet chocolate pieces and
½ cup light corn syrup in a saucepan.
Stir over low heat until chocolate melts.
Add ⅓ cup water. Mix well.
Add 1 teaspoon vanilla.
Cover, refrigerate until cool.*

In large bowl, beat on medium speed 2 cups whipping cream, gradually adding chocolate syrup.
Chill until ready to serve.
Heat 2 quarts milk to scalding. Pour into heated pot.
Fill serving cups half full of chocolate mixture.
Pour in hot milk.
Makes 16-18 servings.

* The chocolate cream probably could be frozen.

FAMILY TIME HOT CHOCOLATE

Our children think it's a great treat on a cold, winter night for us to light a fire in our bedroom fireplace and serve hot chocolate which we make on the dressing room stove. Use your favorite instant chocolate mix, using either hot water or hot milk, and then add a scoop of chocolate ice cream to each mug.
Mmmm ... mmm ... mmm ... good!

Mrs. Lyndon Johnson entertained members of the Congressional Club at the White House on the club's 60th anniversary. She served spiced tea, along with other goodies. When we called the White House social secretary's office they were kind enough to send on the recipe. It's not only delicious, but like anything from the White House, it's historic.

FIRST LADY SPICED TEA

6 teaspoons tea leaves
2 cups boiling water
Pour water over tea and let cool. Strain and add:
1 small can frozen lemon juice
1 small can frozen orange juice
1 ½ cups sugar
2 quarts water
1 stick cinnamon

Simmer mixture for 20 minutes. If too strong, add water. Add extra sugar to taste. This recipe makes 12-20 cups.

During the last two years, I have worked at the Suburban Co-operative Nursery School where Theresa and Visko have attended. This is one of several recipes which I learned about on my "duty day". This mix can be stored. The drink is a good pick-me-up at tea time, says Leolyn Barnett in our office, who also had this recipe.

NURSERY SCHOOL TEA MIX

1 jar (14 ounces) Tang
1 ½ cups instant tea (plain)
1 ½ cups sugar
1 teaspoon cinnamon
½ teaspoon cloves

Mix. Use 1-2 teaspoons per 8-ounce cup of hot water.

SUMMER FAVORITE ICED COFFEE

1 cup strong coffee (refrigerate until cold)
2 egg whites
¼ cup sugar
1 pint coffee ice cream
Toasted slivered almonds
½ teaspoon cinnamon

Beat egg whites until frothy. Gradually add ¼ cup sugar. Beat at high speed until meringue forms soft peaks.

Into each of four TALL glasses pour ¼ cup of cold coffee. Spread the meringue equally over the coffee in each glass. Top meringue with ¼ of ice cream, over which you sprinkle the almonds and the cinnamon. Serve with iced teaspoon. This is a wonderful drink for after-dinner guests who might come by to visit.

Breads & Jams

The "red jam" is still important to Marko and we've collected some good new breads. Bread making is much easier now that I have a new high-powered electric mixer with a bread kneading attachment.

APPLE BUTTER

4 quarts apples, sliced
1 quart sweet cider
1 quart water
2 pounds brown sugar
1 teaspoon cinnamon
1 teaspoon allspice
1 teaspoon cloves

Wash and cut up the apples, add the water and boil until soft. Press through food mill or sieve to remove skins and cores. Put apple pulp and sugar into boiling cider. Continue boiling, stirring constantly in a figure eight, to prevent burning. When it thickens, add the spices and cook until thick enough to spread. Seal in sterilized jars.
Makes about 10 pints.

This is a good "Pennsylvania Dutch" recipe.

My mother always seemed to have more bananas on hand than we could eat before they became too ripe. Like mother, like daughter!

BABA'S BANANA BREAD

¾ cup sugar
2 tablespoons shortening (vegetable oil)
2 eggs, well beaten
3 medium ripe bananas
2 tablespoons sour milk or buttermilk
2 cups flour
1 teaspoon soda
Pinch salt
¼ teaspoon lemon rind

Cream shortening and sugar. Add eggs, mashed ripe bananas, lemon rind. Sift dry ingredients and add alternately with milk. Pour into greased loaf pan. Bake at 350° for 45 minutes.

Makes 1 large loaf.

This recipe has been in my file for 20 years. Bob Voigt taught art and seventh grade when I started as a new teacher at Parrish Junior High School in Salem. Bob used to bring this loaf for an extra treat for those of us who ate our lunch in the teachers' lunchroom. I'd give this an A+ grade any time of year.

BOB VOIGT'S ORANGE BREAD

Place in measuring cup pulp and juice from 2 medium oranges. Add warm water to make 1 fluid cup.
Put orange rinds through fine food chopper and add to juice and pulp in mixing bowl.

Add 2 tablespoons melted shortening
1 beaten egg
¾ cup sugar

Sift in 2 cups flour
½ teaspoon salt
1 ½ teaspoons baking powder
½ teaspoon soda

Add ½ cup chopped nut meats.
Stir only until well-mixed.

Bake in greased and floured loaf pan 1 hour and 10 minutes at 350°.

When Mark was governor, we took a trade mission to Germany. On the return trip, Mrs. E. S. Benjamin, of Salem, and I were "talking recipes." High over the Atlantic she wrote out this recipe for me. It's been high on our list of favorites ever since.

BUTTERMILK PANCAKES

3 ½ to 4 cups flour
2 tablespoons baking powder
1 teaspoon salt
1 quart buttermilk
1 package dry yeast
2 tablespoons baking soda
⅓ cup oil
⅓ cup corn syrup
6 eggs, well beaten

Sift flour, baking powder and salt into large mixing bowl. Add 1 quart buttermilk, sprinkle soda and yeast over batter. Add oil and corn syrup, fold in eggs. Cover and put on bottom shelf of refrigerator overnight. Set out 10 minutes before using. Pour on hot griddle.

This very special Pear Preserve recipe was sent to me via Mary Jane Dellenback. Thank you, Mrs. Herman.

ELLA HERMAN'S PEAR PRESERVES

Peel and dice firm ripe Bartlett pears. To 5 cups of diced pears add 5 cups sugar, ¼ cup cinnamon (red hots) candies and ¼ cup lemon juice. Cook pears, sugar, candies and lemon juice to a rolling boil, stirring constantly with a wooden spoon for 20-25 minutes. Add 1 tablespoon pectin, dissolved in 2 tablespoons water in the last 5-7 minutes. Seal in hot sterilized jars.

Mrs. Herman says to check the time for boiling. Twenty minutes may be better, as it is easy to overcook. Also, less time could make it less firm. She also says not to let the pears and sugar stand to draw out the juice before starting to cook, because they make their own juice quickly when you start to heat them.

EVER-READY BRAN MUFFINS

2 cups boiling water
2 cups pure bran
1 heaping cup shortening
2½ cups sugar
4 beaten eggs
1 quart buttermilk
5 cups sifted flour
5 teaspoons soda
1 teaspoon salt
4 cups all-bran cereal

Pour boiling water over pure bran. Cream sugar and shortening. Add eggs, buttermilk and soaked bran. Sift together flour, salt and soda. Add all bran cereal.
Stir until moistened. Bake at 400° for 15 minutes.
Dates, nuts or fruits may be added.
Mix can be stored in refrigerator until ready to use.

*Ann Reisman, one of my closest Washington friends, gave me this recipe. Since she is associated with **Harper's Bazaar** and is my "fashion counselor," I call these "Fashion Crackers." A new twist for an old-style cracker.*

FASHION CRACKERS

A good accessory for any soup or salad.

20 soda crackers
½ cup water
12 ice cubes, cracked

Place crackers in shallow pan. Cover with cracked ice and water. Let stand until crackers absorb water. Remove crackers to dry cookie sheet. Bake in hot (400 to 450°) oven 30 to 45 minutes, or until puffed and crisp. When puffed and crisp clear through, dab each cracker wihth about ½ teaspoon butter. Return to oven until butter is melted.

Note: It is *very important* to remove crackers to dry pan before baking.

*Jeryme English's popular column, "seen and heard," appears in the Sunday **Oregon Statesman**. I "saw" (and tasted) these delicious biscuits at a dinner party which Jeryme and her husband, Wheeler, hosted for us and I "heard" from Mark that they were absolutely the most delicious and the lightest biscuits he had ever tasted. What else to do but get the recipe ... Mine are not as light as Jeryme's!*

JERYME'S "SEEN AND HEARD" BISCUITS

2 cups sifted flour
4 teaspoons baking powder
¾ teaspoon salt
4 tablespoons shortening
¾ cup milk

Sift together dry ingredients. Cut in shortening. Stir in milk. Turn out on lightly floured board. Knead about ½ minute. Roll dough about ½ inch thick. Cut with 2-inch biscuit cutter. Bake on ungreased baking sheet in hot oven (475°) about 12 minutes.

*On rare occasions I have had to "stand in"
for my husband. On one such occasion, when
he was called back to the Senate for a vote,
I gave a speech at a Thanksgiving Service in
Stayton, Oregon. My thanks to Kay Cook,
who handed me this recipe that night.*

KAY COOK'S PUMPKIN BREAD

Combine:
4 cups sugar
3 cups pumpkin
1 cup oil
3 eggs
1 teaspoon cinnamon
1 teaspoon cloves
1 teaspoon salt

Add:
5 cups flour, sifted with 4 teaspoons soda
2 cups chopped dates or candied fruit
2 cups chopped nuts

Pour into greased loaf-sized bread pans and bake at
350° for 1 hour.

Makes three large loaves, or five small ones.

Barbara Bowles, a long-time school friend of Mark's, moved to Salem when her husband, Chuck, was appointed coach of the track team at Willamette University. Barbara, or B.J., as she is known, is one of those rare good cooks who can produce anything, with or without a recipe. One year for my birthday she brought me a Lemon Bubble Loaf, hot out of her oven. A real treat, and how thoughtful! One doesn't mind getting older with such nice gestures to help ease the pain.

LEMON BUBBLE LOAF

1 cup granulated sugar
¼ teaspoon mace
Grated rind of two lemons
1 cup milk
1 teaspoon salt
¼ cup butter or margarine
½ cup very warm water
3 packages active dry or cake yeast
2 eggs, well beaten
5 ¾ to 6 ¼ cups sifted flour
2 tablespoons melted butter or margarine

Combine first three ingredients, using only ½ cup sugar and set aside this mixture. Scald milk. Stir in remaining ½ cup sugar, salt, ¼ cup butter. Cool until lukewarm. In large bowl, measure very warm water, sprinkle in yeast, stir until dissolved. Stir in milk mix, eggs, and 3 cups flour and enough to make a soft dough that just cleans sides of bowl. Sprinkle board with flour, turn dough out on it and knead until smooth, elastic with small blisters under surface. Place in large greased bowl, turn to coat all sides, cover with towel, let rise until double. Poke fingers into dough and punch down. Turn dough onto floured surface, cover, let rest 10 minutes. Grease angel loaf pan, 15 ½" long. Cut dough into 16 equal pieces. Shape pieces into balls, tucking ends under. Place in layer in pan, brush with half of melted butter, sprinkle with half lemon mix. Repeat second layer. Let rise until double. Bake at 350° for 35 minutes, or until done. Cool in pan five minutes, then turn out onto wire racks.

*How fortunate we are to have John Ober-
dorf as our "field man" in our home office
in Salem.   And, as is the case with many
public servants, we get "two for the price
of one." Lois Oberdorf is charming, concerned, dedicated, and a good citizen who
is also a good wife, mother and cook. It's
always great fun to "break bread" with
Lois and John, and Lois usually has a new
kind of bread each time.*

LOIS OBERDORF'S MONKEY BREAD

1 cake compressed yeast
1 cup milk, scalded and cooled to lukewarm
4 tablespoons sugar
1 teaspoon salt
½ cup melted butter
About 3 ½ cups sifted flour
Additional melted butter

In a large bowl, dissolve yeast in lukewarm milk.
Stir in sugar, salt, ½ cup butter, and flour. Beat
well, cover, and let rise in a warm place until almost doubled in bulk (about 1 hour). Punch down
and roll out on a lightly floured board to ¼-inch
thickness. Cut into diamond-shaped pieces about
2 ½ inches long.

Dip each piece in melted butter and arrange in
overlapping layers in a 9-inch ring mold — mold
should be about half full. Let rise until almost
doubled in bulk. Bake in a hot oven (400°) for 30
minutes or until golden brown.

Serves 12.

From Marilyn Isaac of our staff comes this delicious recipe for "Crescent Rolls."

MARILYN'S CRESCENT ROLLS

Dissolve 2 cakes yeast in a small amount of warm water (¼ cup), scald 1 cup milk and then cool to lukewarm. To this add 3 well-beaten eggs and ½ cup sugar, 1 teaspoon salt and 4 cups flour (you may need a little more flour). Knead thoroughly and let rise until double in bulk. Then divide dough in fourths and roll each portion as a pie crust. Brush with melted butter (½ cube) and cut in pie-shaped wedges. Roll each pie-shaped wedge, beginning with the wide edge. Place on greased cookie sheet 2 inches apart and let rise again. Bake in preheated oven at 350° until brown (about 12 to 18 minutes).

Important: Lay pointed part of each roll down, so rolls won't come open while rising.

*From the wonderful high country of East-
ern Oregon, and Mrs. Irvin Mann, Jr.,
(whose husband serves in the State Legislature) comes this . . .*

BATTER BREAD

1 package dry yeast
½ cup warm water
⅛ teaspoon ground ginger
3 tablespoons sugar
1 teaspoon salt
2 tablespoons salad oil
4-4 ½ cups flour (unsifted)
1 can evaporated milk

Dissolve yeast in water; blend in ginger and 1
tablespoon sugar. Let stand until bubbly (15
minutes). Stir in 2 tablespoons sugar, milk, salt,
salad oil. Beat in flour, 1 cup at a time. Add until
dough is heavy, too sticky to knead. Place dough
in greased 2-pound coffee tin or two 1-pound coffee
tins, or loaf pans. Let stand until batter rises above
top of can (45-60 minutes). Bake at 350° for 45
minutes for 1-pound cans, 60 for 2-pound cans.
Brush top with butter. Cool 5-10 minutes. Take
out and cool on rack.

*These are great — morning, noon or night!
A recipe from the children's piano teacher.*

MRS. GIBBENS' MUSICAL MUFFINS

Combine and soak 15 minutes:
1 cup buttermilk
1 cup quick oatmeal

Combine:
1 cup flour
1 teaspoon baking powder
½ teaspoon soda
½ teaspoon salt
⅓ cup melted shortening
⅓ cup brown sugar
1 beaten egg

Mix all together. Bake 20 minutes in greased muffin tins, at 400°. Yield: 12 muffins.

*There is something about the aroma of gingerbread baking that makes any house smell like a warm and friendly **home.** Try this and see.*

MY BEST GINGERBREAD

½ cup sugar
½ cup butter
1 egg
1 cup molasses
2 ½ cups sifted flour
1 ½ teaspoon soda
1 teaspoon cinnamon
1 teaspoon ginger
½ teaspoon cloves
½ teaspoon salt
1 cup hot water

Cream butter and sugar. Add beaten eggs, molasses, then dry ingredients which have been sifted together. Add hot water last and beat until smooth. The batter is soft, but it makes a fine cake. Bake in greased, shallow pan 35 minutes, in moderate oven (325-350°). Makes 15 generous portions.

SAUCE FOR CREPES OR HOT CAKES

2 egg yolks
1 cup milk
½ cup granulated sugar
½ cup brown sugar
½ cup water
1 teaspoon vanilla
2 pieces lemon or orange peel

Cook all together, stirring well on medium heat until it begins to thicken. Cool and remove peel. Place in center of crepe — roll up. Sprinkle with powdered sugar.

Bert and Christine Keith have been on our campaign team for years. Bert has as many cookbooks as I do, and when we don't agree on political issues, we can talk recipes.

SCOTCH SCONES

2 cups flour
½ teaspoon salt
1 teaspoon sugar
1 teaspoon cream of tartar
1 teaspoon soda
3 cups buttermilk, sour milk or sour cream

Sift dry ingredients together. Take 1 cup and mix with enough liquid to make a soft dough. Pat out until about ½ to ¾ -inch thick. Cut in triangles, squares or rounds. Bert says to bake them on floured griddle on top of stove, turning when brown, to brown on other side. And he finds that in most cases the flour on the scones is sufficient for the griddle. I prefer to bake in a 400° oven 8-10 minutes or until brown.

*It pays to know your food editor. Marian Burros of the **Washington Evening Star** came to my rescue when I looked for a similar corn bread recipe which I had in my files, and had promised to send to some visiting postal employees, but couldn't find the recipe. Thanks, Marian.*

SPANISH CORN BREAD

1 cup buttermilk
1 cup yellow corn meal
1 cup presifted flour
3 teaspoons sugar
1 teaspoon salt
1 teaspoon baking powder
½ teaspoon baking soda
1 egg, lightly beaten
¼ cup melted shortening
8-ounce can whole-kernel corn, drained
4-ounce can roasted green peppers, drained and chopped
4-ounce can pimientos, drained and chopped
2 cups grated cheddar cheese

In small mixing bowl, combine buttermilk and corn meal. Let stand for 30 minutes.

Preheat oven to 375°. Grease 13 x 9 ½ x 2-inch pan. Into large mixing bowl, sift together dry ingredients. Add egg, shortening and corn meal mixture. Stir well. Add corn, green peppers and pimientos. Stir well. Add cheese. Mix well. Turn batter into pan. Bake in preheated oven for 30 minutes.

Serves eight to ten, and tastes best when served warm.

One needn't worry about entertaining a "celebrity" if they are all as nice and appreciative as Pianist Van Cliburn. One year Van and Mark celebrated their mutual July 12 birthday here in Washington the night before Van opened the Merriweather Post Pavillion in Columbia, Maryland. The Pavillion is the summer home of the Washington National Symphony Orchestra.

This Spoon Bread is more like a soufflé, so don't worry if it falls . . . the flavor remains, and so will the extra pounds if you eat too much. As you can tell, the helpings he had don't show on the slender Mr. Cliburn.

VAN CLIBURN SPOON BREAD

2 cups milk, scalded
1 cup corn meal
1 teaspoon salt
2 cubes butter
1 teaspoon sugar
⅛ teaspoon dillweed
½ teaspoon onion flakes
5 egg yolks, beaten very light
5 egg whites, beaten stiff, but not dry

Gradually stir corn meal into hot milk; add salt. Cook to mush stage, while stirring constantly. Remove from heat; add butter and sugar, dillweed and onion flakes. Stir until butter melts; cool.

Add egg yolks to cooled mush. Fold in whites. Pour into 2-quart casserole. Bake at 350° (it will puff up like a soufflé), for 45 minutes to one hour. Serve immediately; serves eight to ten.

Dorotha Wilbut, Iris Collins, Aunt Dorothy and I went to one of those health spas a number of years ago. We called it the "Fat Farm" and ever since have looked for not-so-fattening recipes. Dorotha found this one, but since the new ruling on cyclamates by the Department of Health, Education and Welfare, I'm not sure how much "thinner" this syrup will be.

WAISTLINE WAFFLES

In a saucepan, heat syrup drained from one 16-ounce can of dietetic apricots. Dissolve 1 tablespoon cornstarch in juice of ½ lemon; stir into hot syrup until thickened and clear. Stir in apricots, coarsely chopped.

In large bowl, sift ¾ cup sifted cake flour, 2 teaspoons baking powder, ¾ teaspoon salt and 1 teaspoon sugar. Add 1 cup skim milk, 2 egg yolks and 1 tablespoon melted margarine. Beat until smooth. Fold in 2 stiffly beaten egg whites. Bake in waffle iron. Makes two to eight waffles. Quarter and serve with hot sauce.

Elaine Ogden, one of the Co-operative Nursery School mothers, helped the 4-year-old class make this bread one day and bake it the next. We all hoped that the bread baking day would fall on our "duty day." Elaine calls it easy and foolproof. Try it and you'll agree.

WONDERFUL NURSERY SCHOOL BREAD

Stir together in *large* bowl and let cool to lukewarm:
2 cups boiling water
⅓ to ½ cup sugar
1 tablespoon salt
⅓ cup butter or margarine

Place in measuring cup and allow to rise to the top of the cup:
2 packages dry yeast
1 teaspoon sugar
¼ cup warm water

Add 2 well-beaten eggs and yeast mixture to the large bowl mixture of water, sugar and butter. Mix well. Add 4 cups *unsifted flour* — mix until smooth. Add 4 more cups *unsifted flour* and mix until all flour is incorporated.

Cover with plastic bowl cover and refrigerate until double in size — about 2 to 3 hours. (Elaine says you can keep the dough refrigerated up to 8 days.)

Divide dough into 3 parts, knead lightly and shape into loaves and put into 3 loaf pans, or shape into rolls. Cover with towel and let rise in a warm place until double in size — 1 to 1 ½ hours. Heat oven to 350° — place loaves in middle of oven and reduce heat to 325°.

Cakes

In the last book we apologized to Betty Crocker, Duncan Hines and Pillsbury. In this book we are grateful to them, as many of these recipes have as their basis a "mix."

*From Marian Lowry Fischer, the long-time food editor of the **Capitol Journal**, in Salem, comes this recipe. Marian, for years, always let me have "advance" copies of her food editors' conference recipes. I miss those now.*

AUTUMN ANGEL

Heat oven to 375°. Prepare Tropical Mist Angel Food cake mix as directed on package, except add ½ cup of prepared mincemeat during the last half minute of mixing. Do not overblend. Fold through mixture several times to distribute mincemeat evenly. Pour into pan. Bake 35-45 minutes. Invert on funnel or bottle. Cool. Frost cake with orange glaze.

Orange Glaze:
Blend 4¾ cups sifted confectioners' sugar, 1 tablespoon grated orange peel, ¼ cup orange juice, 2 tablespoons orange flavoring and 1-2 drops yellow food coloring thoroughly. (If needed, add 1-2 teaspoons more orange juice.)

Cynthia Baker Sharp was one of my resident assistant colleagues when we were both doing our graduate work at Stanford University. Because Cynthia was such a marvelous writer and wit, we hardly ever believed she'd settle down to a kitchen. What fun it was to find her living in Washington when we arrived — settled in not only her kitchen, but the PTA, the neighborhood newspaper, politics, and any other civic group that needed her. I was sorry when her husband's railroad career sent them to Chicago, via Minneapolis. She tells me there are no private railroad cars for railroad vice presidents, just executive jets! Her recipe for coffee cake is really superb.

CYNTHIA SHARP'S CHRISTMAS EVE COFFEE CAKE

Cynthia says, "This is not tree-shaped (it could be), not even green; but it's so easy to make and yet 'special' enough for Christmas morning, that my mother always made it on Christmas Eve."

2 cups flour
2 teaspoons baking powder
¼ teaspoon nutmeg
½ teaspoon cinnamon
¼ teaspoon salt
½ teaspoon soda
1 cup sugar
1 cup sour milk
1 beaten egg
Add 2 teaspoons melted butter

Mix ingredients and pour into 9 x 13-inch pan. Then sprinkle with ½ cup sugar mixed with cinnamon. Dot with butter. Bake 20 minutes at 350°.

And, speaking of calories, June's Chocolate Refrigerator Cake has its share. June sat in front of me at a James Beard Cooking Demonstration in Portland and we agreed to exchange some of our own recipes — even if they might not be as well-known as those of that day's lecturer.

CHOCOLATE REFRIGERATOR CAKE

4 ounces sweet chocolate
1 envelope unflavored gelatin
2 tablespoons cold water
¼ cup strong coffee, boiling
5 egg yolks, well beaten
⅛ teaspoon salt
1 teaspoon vanilla
5 egg whites, beaten
½ cup powdered sugar
1 cup whipping cream
2 dozen lady fingers

Topping:
1 cup whipping cream
1 tablespoon rum flavoring
Shaved chocolate curls

Melt chocolate in double boiler. Soften gelatin in cold water and dissolve in the hot coffee. Beat egg yolks with salt and vanilla. Add to chocolate and cook a few minutes over simmering water, stirring constantly. Stir in gelatin. Cool; but before mixture begins to set, fold in egg whites which have been beaten with powdered sugar. Fold in the whipped cream. Line bottom and sides of a spring-form pan with lady fingers. Fill with chocolate mixture. (You can use any extra lady fingers in the filling.) Chill. Before serving cover with 1 cup cream, whipped with rum flavoring added and slightly sweetened. Decorate with shaved chocolate curls. Serves 10 to 12.

Cakes

Helen Gatewood and I shared an apart-
ment as new, young teachers in Salem.
Spiced Crumb Cake is one of her good solid
recipes for family-time eating. Both
Helen and I loved to cook when we weren't
grading papers or preparing lesson plans.

SPICED CRUMB CAKE

2 cups cake flour
1 teaspoon soda
1 cup sugar
1 ½ teaspoons cinnamon
1 teaspoon cloves
¼ teaspoon allspice
¼ teaspoon salt
½ cup shortening
1 egg, well beaten
2 tablespoons molasses
1 cup sour milk or buttermilk

Cream shortening, sugar and molasses. Add well-
beaten egg. Add dry ingredients and milk alternately.
Pour in small, square, greased cake pan.

Make crumb mixture of:
2 tablespoons butter, melted
1 tablespoon flour
4 teaspoons sugar
½ teaspoon cinnamon
Sprinkle above mixture over cake batter. Bake 40 to
45 minutes at 350°. This cake is best warm and un-
frosted.

***Look alikes**—The following recipes use a package mix, 4 eggs, ½ to ¾ cup oil, and a variation on a theme ingredient. Anita Bryant served us the Florida Citrus Cake recipe when we were in Miami for the 1968 Republican Convention. Besides being a glamorous singer, she is a wonderful homemaker and mother and devout Christian layworker.*

GRETCHEN QUIE'S ANNAPOLIS CAKE

1 package lemon cake mix
4 eggs
½ cup sugar
½ cup oil
1 jar Junior food apricots, or 1 cup pureed apricots

Blend and beat for 2 minutes. Grease and flour tube pan. Bake at 350° for 45-50 minutes.

Glaze while warm, in pan, using ice pick to puncture top of cake.

Glaze:
1 cup powdered sugar combined with juice of 1 lemon.

FLORIDA CITRUS CAKE — FROM ANITA BRYANT

4 eggs
1 package yellow cake mix
1 package instant lemon pudding
¾ cup water
¾ cup vegetable oil

Put all ingredients in the mixer at once and beat well. Pour into a greased tube pan. Bake 50 minutes or until done, at 325°. Ice cake in pan while still hot, with 1 ½ cups powdered sugar, 2 tablespoons butter and ⅓ cup of concentrated orange juice. Let cool. Then take out of pan.

Cakes

NUTMEG ANGEL CAKE
WITH PRALINE FROSTING

1 cup sifted cake flour
½ cup sugar
¾ teaspoon ground nutmeg
1 ¼ cups (about 10 or 11 large) egg whites
¼ teaspoon salt
1 ¼ teaspoons cream of tartar
1 cup sugar
1 teaspoon pure vanilla extract

Sift cake flour; add the ½ cup sugar and nutmeg and
sift again. In a separate bowl, beat egg whites and
salt until foamy. Sprinkle cream of tartar over mixture and continue beating until egg whites form soft
peaks. They should be moist and glossy. Sprinkle the
1 cup sugar, 2 tablespoons at a time, over egg whites.
Fold in gently, but thoroughly, after each addition.
Sift flour mixture, approximately ¼ cup at a time,
over mixture. Fold in gently after each addition.
Fold in pure vanilla extract. Turn into ungreased
10-inch tube pan and bake in preheated moderate
oven (375°) for 40 minutes or until a cake tester
inserted in the center comes out clean. Invert pan on
rack and cool. When completely cool, remove from
pan and ice with Praline Frosting.

Praline Frosting:
2 tablespoons butter or margarine
⅓ cup heavy cream
⅔ cup light brown sugar, firmly packed
⅛ teaspoon salt
⅛ teaspoon cream of tartar
¼ teaspoon pure vanilla extract
About 2 cups sifted confectioners' sugar
⅔ cup coarsely chopped walnuts

In a saucepan, combine first five ingredients. Bring to
a boil, stirring constantly. Remove from heat and
add pure vanilla extract and enough confectioners'
sugar to make of spreading consistency. Spread
frosting on top of cake, allowing some of it to run
down sides. Garnish top with chopped walnuts.
Yields one 10-inch cake.

*The Praline frosting is what makes this cake
unique. If you need a shortcut, use a packaged
angel cake mix — I do!*

In the "good old days" at Willamette University, in Salem, we had many friends among the faculty. Dean Gregg's wife, Lois, was also an active political supporter. Here is a marvelous recipe using a good Oregon product—prunes.

OREGON PRUNE CAKE

Sift together in a bowl:
2 cups all-purpose flour
1 ½ cups sugar
½ teaspoon salt
1 teaspoon soda
1 teaspoon cinnamon
¼ teaspoon nutmeg
¼ teaspoon allspice

Add:
1 cup vegetable oil
1 cup buttermilk
1 tablespoon vanilla
Beat until smooth, about 2 minutes. Add 3 eggs and beat 2 minutes. Add 1 cup chopped nuts, 1 cup cooked prunes, cut up. Bake in a 9 x 13-inch pan for 45 minutes at 350°. Perforate, while hot, with a toothpick.

Bring to a boil:
1 cup sugar
½ cup buttermilk
1 tablespoon corn syrup
1 teaspoon vanilla
½ stick margarine

Pour gently over cake. Serve warm with whipped cream, or just "as is."

Freezes well.

Two of the many outstanding supporters on our political team are Otto and Marabel Frohnmayer of Medford. Through thick and thin they stand firm . . . the best kind of friends any public servant can have. Here is a delicious recipe from Marabel.

PINEAPPLE CARROT CAKE

4 eggs, beaten in large bowl
2 cups grated carrots
1 cup crushed pineapple and juice
2 cups sugar
1 cup ground walnuts
1 cup oil
2 ½ cups flour
1 teaspoon soda
1 teaspoon baking powder
2 teaspoons cinnamon

Mix ingredients and bake in three layers, or large loaf pan. Bake at 350° for 40 minutes, or until tester comes out clean.

Frosting:
1 package (8 ounces) cream cheese
¼ pound margarine
1 package (1 pound) powdered sugar
(Drained, crushed pineapple may be added, if desired.)

*Here is another variation on the angel food
cake theme. It's good for serving around
Halloween time.*

PUMPKIN ANGEL

1 can (1 pound) pumpkin
3 teaspoons pumpkin pie spice
¼ cup light brown sugar, firmly packed
1 package (14 ½ ounces) angel food cake mix
1 ⅓ cups water
2 tablespoons butter or margarine, melted
1 quart vanilla ice cream, slightly softened
Assorted candies
½ teaspoon vanilla extract
1 to 2 tablespoons milk
1 ½ cups sifted confectioners' sugar

Blend together ¾ cup pumpkin, 1 ½ teaspoons pumpkin pie spice and 2 tablespoons brown sugar; set
aside. Prepare cake mix according to package directions; fold pumpkin mixture into half the batter.
Alternately spoon pumpkin and white batter into an
ungreased 3-quart ring mold; cut through batter with
knife to give marbeled effect. Bake and cool as directed on the package. Meanwhile, combine ¾ cup
pumpkin, 1 ½ teaspoons pumpkin pie spice, remaining brown sugar, and 1 tablespoon butter. Swirl
through ice cream; freeze until serving time. Remove
completely cook cake from pan. Arrange candies on
top of cake. Combine remaining pumpkin and butter
with last three ingredients. Slowly pour glaze over
candies. Pile ice cream in center and serve. Makes
16 servings.

QUICK AND EASY LEMON CHEESECAKE

1 package (8 ounces) cream cheese
2 cups whole milk
1 package lemon instant pudding
9-inch graham cracker crust

Stir cream cheese until very soft; blend in ½ cup milk. Add remaining milk and the pudding mix. Beat slowly with egg beater just until well mixed, about 1 minute. (Do not overbeat.) Pour at once into graham cracker crust. Sprinkle graham cracker crumbs lightly over top. Chill about 1 hour. Serve with whipped cream.

Variation:
Top may be sprinkled with combination of graham cracker crumbs and:
1 teaspoon sugar
¼ teaspoon cinnamon
¼ teaspoon nutmeg

SILVIA'S ALMOND CHOCOLATE CAKE

Bake dark chocolate cake mix in two layers, as package directs. When cool, split each layer in two and fill with the following mixture:

Beat in mixing bowl:
¼ pound butter
1 pound confectioners' sugar
3 or 4 tablespoons milk
4 tablespoons instant cocoa

In butter, fry almonds (2¾ ounce package). Fill layers with filling; sprinkle with nuts, saving enough for top. Assemble layers and frost with the following topping:
Whip 2 packages whipped topping
Add 2 tablespoons instant cocoa
Add 3 teaspoons instant coffee
Sprinkle with remaining almonds

"Magnifique" is none too good a word for this cake. Silvia Zimmerman tried to teach me French before her State Department husband was reassigned to Portugal. Silvia and I talked more about recipes than French, but it was fun.

Cookies

*"It still takes a Heap of Cookies" to make
a House a Home . . ."*

A fond memory of college was tea time on Sunday nights at the Alpha Phi House. Anna, our cook, had been there through two generations of Alpha Phis, and every Sunday night we knew there would be two large pans of "Anna's Brownies." I'm glad I was able to get the recipe from her some years later.

ANNA'S ALPHA PHI CHEWY CHOCOLATE BROWNIES

2 squares bitter chocolate (melted)
½ cup butter (melted)
2 eggs
1 cup sugar
Pinch of salt
1 teaspoon vanilla
½ cup flour
1 cup nut meats

Beat eggs, add sugar, beat again. Add melted chocolate and butter, vanilla, salt and sifted flour, and mix until smooth. Add nut meats. Pour into greased 9 x 12-inch pan. Bake in moderate oven at 350° for 30 minutes.

Yield: 24

*In ReMARKable Recipes, you saw many of Iris Collins' recipes, but here is one which is a favorite of young and old alike. You just have to plan ahead on these cookies because the oatmeal **must** be soaked overnight.*

AUNTIE IRIS' OATMEAL COOKIES

4 cups quick-cooking oats, soaked overnight in
1 cup melted butter. In morning add:
2 beaten eggs
2 cups brown sugar
¼ teaspoon salt
1 teaspoon vanilla
1 cup chopped nut meats

Drop on greased cookie sheet with teaspoon. Bake 15 minutes at 350°.

This is a Yugoslav sweet that was always in evidence in my home during the holiday season. They are heavy and can be a bit greasy if not properly drained.

BABA'S PRSURATE

Boil 9 medium-size potatoes until done. Reserve water and mash well. Add 2 teaspoons salt, mix with a little water saved from boiling potatoes, in bottom of pan. Add:

4 cups sugar
1 pound seedless raisins
6 apples, well chopped
2 cups chopped walnuts
1 teaspoon allspice
1 teaspoon nutmeg
1 teaspoon cinnamon
4-6 ounces grape juice
2 ounces anise extract
1 tablespoon vanilla
2 lemons, juice and rind
3 oranges, juice and rind (put rind through food chopper)
5 teaspoons baking powder
4-5 cups all-purpose flour (add more flour as needed)

Beat well, fry walnut-size bits of dough in deep hot vegetable oil (375°). Drain on paper towels.

Baba says, "Better yet, get an extra pair of hands to help beat batter. It takes quite a bit of beating. This makes a huge batch. I've never cut it down because you can freeze them and once you've gone to the trouble of mixing you may as well make plenty. I never had many left to freeze, but tried freezing a dozen and they turned out all right."

When Mrs. Harry Holt of Creswell, Oregon, was named American Mother of the Year, I had a tea in her honor. These cookies were among those served that day.

BROWN SUGAR DROPS

1 cup soft shortening
2 cups brown sugar (packed)
2 eggs
½ cup buttermilk
3 ½ cups sifted flour
1 teaspoon soda
1 teaspoon salt

Mix shortening, brown sugar and eggs thoroughly. Stir in milk; sift together flour, soda and salt and stir in. Chill at least 1 hour. Heat oven to 375°. Drop rounded teaspoonfuls of dough about 2 inches apart on lightly greased baking sheet. Bake 8 to 10 minutes, or until no imprint remains when touched lightly with finger.
Makes about 6 dozen 2 ½ inch cookies.

Variation:
To fill: Place ½ teaspoon date filling on dough and cover with ½ teaspoonful of dough. Bake 10 to 12 minutes, until lightly browned.

Date Filling:
2 cups dates, finely cut up or ground
¾ cup water
¾ cup sugar
½ cup chopped nuts

Cook fruit, sugar and water together slowly, stirring constantly until thickened. Add nuts, cool. Makes about 2 ½ cups of filling.

Camille Pappert was my right hand during the years Mark was governor. When Camille was in the kitchen during a party, I didn't have to worry. Things always went smoothly. She has since passed away, but in her memory I present here one of her best cookie recipes.

GRANDMA'S SUGAR COOKIES

1 ¾ cups sugar
1 cup butter
Pinch salt
4 egg yolks and 2 whole eggs
4 cups flour
1 teaspoon soda
2 teaspoons baking powder
1 tablespoon vanilla
1 cup sweet milk

Cream sugar and butter. Add salt and eggs and blend well. Add flour and milk to this and mix well. Chill thoroughly. Roll and cut in fancy shapes. A little flour may be added so you can roll the dough. Decorate or sprinkle with sugar or frost cookies after baking. Bake at 375° for about 10 minutes. Do not grease pan.

Frosting:
1 ½ cups powdered sugar
⅛ teaspoon cream of tartar
1 egg white
1 teaspoon vanilla

Beat in electric mixer until frosting holds its shape. Cover with damp cloth when not in use.

If you are in that "over thirty" bracket, many of you may have around your mother's copy of **Household Searchlight Cookbook** *which was a favorite in the "thirties." My first cooking try was with the chocolate cookie recipe that follows from the pages of that book.*

CHOCOLATE COOKIES

6 tablespoons butter or butter substitute
1 ½ squares unsweetened chocolate
6 tablespoons milk
⅓ teaspoon baking soda
¼ teaspoon salt
1 teaspoon baking powder
1 ⅛ cups flour
¾ cup sugar
1 egg, well beaten
¾ cup chopped nuts
1 teaspoon vanilla

Melt chocolate over hot water. Cream butter and sugar. Add chocolate and egg. Mix thoroughly. Sift flour, measure, and sift with soda, baking powder and salt. Add alternately with milk to first mixture. Add flavoring and nuts. Mix thoroughly. Drop by teaspoonfuls on well-greased baking sheet. Bake in hot oven (400°) for 10-12 minutes.
Makes 30 cookies. If desired, cookies may be iced.

Iris Collins' and Pat Reger's Seven Layered Cookies have been called "Emergency Cookies" and were responsible for one of the best friendships I have made since coming to Washington. Marian Burros, who is now food editor for the **Washington Evening Star,** *came to interview me shortly after we arrived in Washington. The message that she wanted to take pictures of something I had cooked did not reach me. We were both on a tight schedule. When I produced Seven Layer Cookies, with some substitute ingredients, she (I, too) was amazed at the immediate results. Needless to say, they are a cinch to make and never fail, and no mess in the kitchen.*

EMERGENCY COOKIES

1 cube butter
1 ½ cups graham cracker crumbs
1 package (6 ounces) butterscotch bits
1 package (6 ounces) chocolate chips
1 package (6 ½ ounces) coconut
1 cup chopped nuts
1 can (15 ounces) sweetened, condensed milk

Melt butter in 9 x 12-inch pan. Stir in cracker crumbs. Add butterscotch bits, chocolate chips, coconut and nuts. Dribble milk over all.
Bake at 350° for 25 minutes.

The recipe for these Coconut Bars comes from Ethel Ziegler, who was affectionately called "Mom" during the years her husband served Benton County, Oregon in the House and Senate of the State Legislature.

COCONUT BARS

½ cup butter
1 cup flour

Mix and pat into 9 x 12-inch pan. Bake at 350° for 10 minutes.

1 ½ cups brown sugar
½ cup coconut
1 cup chopped nuts
2 tablespoons flour
½ teaspoon salt
2 eggs
1 teaspoon vanilla
¼ teaspoon baking powder

Mix and spread over butter and flour mixture after it has cooled slightly. Return to oven and bake 20 minutes at 350°.

Cool and frost with:
1 ½ cups powdered sugar
2 tablespoons orange juice
2 tablespoons butter
1 tablespoon lemon juice

Cut into bars to serve.

Gretchen McNeese, an old college friend with whom I correspond at Christmas and on our birthdays, sent me this Filbert Cookie recipe because she knew I am always looking for recipes which use Oregon products. Gretchen and her husband now live in Chicago. I'll bet they miss Oregon, too.

GRETCHEN'S FILBERT COOKIES

4 eggs
1 pound powdered sugar
1 pound filberts, grated almost as fine as flour
(should be able to do this in a blender) (about 3-4
cups ground nuts)
¼ teaspoon salt
1 ½ to 2 teaspoons grated lemon rind

Beat the eggs very well, then add other ingredients.
Chill dough at least 1 hour. Drop by teaspoonfuls
onto greased cookie sheet and bake about 20 minutes
at 375°.

Store in tight metal containers with a piece of bread
to keep them moist.

JELLY TOTS

½ cup melted butter
1 ½ tablespoons sugar
1 cup finely chopped filbert meats
½ teaspoon grated lemon rind
1 teaspoon vanilla
Sift and stir in 1 ½ cups bread flour

Place the bowl over hot water so that the dough will become soft enough to handle. Form into little balls and imprint with your thumb. Put jam or jelly of your choice in the center. Bake at 400° for 10 minutes. Sprinkle with confectioners' sugar.

Makes 18-24 small party cookies — that melt in your mouth.

Jenny, Aunt Dorothy Cook's housekeeper, has given me many good recipes. Here's one which can be served for breakfast or brunch.

SCOTCH OATCAKES

2 cups oatmeal
½ cup sifted flour
¼ teaspoon salt
¼ teaspoon soda
1 teaspoon sugar
½ cup butter or margarine
1 cup boiling water

Combine oatmeal, flour, salt, soda, sugar and blend well. Add butter to boiling water and stir until butter is melted. Stir into oatmeal mixture until blended and set aside to cool. When cool, turn mixture onto lightly floured board and roll out ⅛-inch thick. Cut with biscuit cutter or knife into squares and place on cookie sheet.
Bake at 400° for 5-8 minutes or until lightly browned.

Makes 2 dozen 2-inch cakes.

*This is another childhood favorite which my
mother used to make at Christmas and Easter.*

KRUSTULE

12 eggs
12 tablespoons sugar
12 tablespoons oil
12 tablespoons orange juice
1 tablespoon vanilla or anise
1 pinch salt
3 cups flour

Beat eggs until quite thick (10 minutes with electric
beater). Add sugar, oil, flavoring, orange juice and
salt; beat well. Add enough flour to make dough stiff
enough to barely handle — about 3 cups. Don't knead
too much — roll, then cut in strips and fry in hot
oil. You can fry in deep fryer. Also, tie strip in soft
knot, or just overlap. Fry until they turn a little beige
and turn over for 3 seconds, then drain on paper towel
and sprinkle with powdered sugar.

This recipe can be halved or quartered. If you use 12
eggs, you will be frying all day.
These can be frozen, also.

*One of the ladies who helped in the kitchen
in Salem brought in these cookies. They are
an attractive addition to a cookie platter,
but sometimes the powdered sugar "goes all
over" when they are being eaten.*

LILY COOKIES

Cream 4 ½ ounces cream cheese, 1 cup butter or
shortening and 2 cups sifted flour. Roll out and cut
with 2-inch round cutter. Roll into cornucopias by
bringing two rounded edges together, letting them
overlap. Press them gently; shape like a lily. Fill
open part with a little jelly. Bake at 375° about 15
minutes. Cool and drench with powdered sugar.

The 1925 F Street Club serves some of the best food in Washington. Mrs. John Gross, who owns the club, oversees the operation and is particular about every detail of service. The club seems to be the last of its kind that characterizes that old age of elegance in Washington houses. "Aunt Laura" was good enough to share this recipe. Yes, it does take a hot oven!

LACE COOKIES

3 cups flour (all purpose)
2 ½ cups sugar
¾ pound butter
5 whole eggs
3 tablespoons light cream

Cream butter and sugar together until light and pale. Then add all other ingredients together and beat for 30 minutes with electric beater and chill for one hour. Drop by teaspoonfuls onto cookie sheet and bake at 500° for 4 ½ minutes. Remove from pan immediately and cool on wire rack.

*Both Theresa and Visko had the good for-
tune to have Sally Rosen as their nursery
school teacher. Sally is very creative and
before Christmas each year the children
made and baked their own gingerbread man.*

SALLY'S NURSERY SCHOOL GINGERBREAD MEN

Sift together:
4 cups flour
1 teaspoon salt
1 teaspoon baking powder
1 teaspoon soda
½ teaspoon nutmeg
1 teaspoon ginger
1 teaspoon cinnamon

Mix together:
1 cup butter
1 cup molasses
1 cup sugar
2 egg yolks

Mix the wet and dry ingredients well. Roll on a
floured board. Cut with a cutter. Decorate with
raisins. Put on a greased cookie pan. Bake at 350°
for 8 minutes.

*Elizabeth Lord, who gave me this recipe, was
our neighbor in Salem. Her father was former
Governor William P. Lord, of Oregon.
Elizabeth is as creative in the kitchen as she
and Edith Schryver are in planning gardens.
They are remarkable landscape architects.*

SAND TARTS

½ cup soft butter
1 cup white sugar
1 egg, beaten
2 teaspoons baking powder
1 ¾ cups bread flour
Pinch salt
1 egg white, slightly beaten
1 tablespoon vanilla or lemon extract

Sift flour and baking powder together. Cream butter
and sugar. Add beaten egg. Add flour, baking powder
and salt. Add vanilla or lemon extract. Roll out
dough, place in refrigerator for 1 hour or more.
When dough is firm, roll out as much as you can
handle before it becomes too soft. Smear the top of
the cut cookies with the slightly beaten egg white
and sprinkle a little sugar over the top. Add cinnamon if preferred. This gives an extra brittleness. Bake
at 300° for 15 minutes. Makes 70 cookies, medium
size.

Scotch Shorties are a genuine treat. The real thing came from Aunt Dorothy's Scottish maid's sister, Jean. Jean made them for me to take home to serve at a dinner party the day after one of my trips from California to Washington; but the family found them so tasty I had to whip up a batch myself the afternoon of the party. They go very well with ice cream, fresh fruit, or pudding.

SCOTCH SHORTIES

1 cup all-purpose flour
½ cup corn starch
½ cup powdered sugar
1 cup butter

Put flour, corn starch and sugar in mixing bowl. Add butter and crumble like bread crumbs with dry ingredients. Knead dough until soft texture. Divide into three parts, then roll each on baking sheet until dough fits length of sheet. Then roll in demerara sugar and put in refrigerator until firm. When firm, cut each roll about ½-inch thick and place on greased, floured cookie sheet. Bake approximately 30 minutes in a moderate oven (325°) or until golden brown. Remove from tray immediately and allow to cool.

We were privileged to be guests of the Attorney General and Mrs. Mitchell the night they entertained aboard the Presidential Yacht Sequoia for the pleasure of Senator and Mrs. McClellan of Arkansas. Instead of these brownies, we were served strawberries for dessert, although I am told that for years these brownies were as much a part of the Sequoia as the Presidential Seal in the dining room.

FROM MARIAN BURROS' SEQUOIA BROWNIES

½ pound butter
4 squares bitter chocolate
2 pounds dark brown sugar
1 cup flour
4 eggs
1 tablespoon vanilla
2 cups chopped walnuts
½ teaspoon salt

Melt butter, chocolate and sugar in top of double boiler. Remove from heat and stir in flour and salt. Add eggs, one at a time, beating well between each addition. Stir in remaining ingredients. Line a 1-inch deep cookie pan with wax paper. Pour in brownie mixture. Dot with whole walnuts. Bake at 300° for 45 minutes. Turn off oven and let pan stand in oven for another 15 minutes. Remove and invert pan on flat surface. Peel off wax paper. Let cook one hour and cut in squares.

DO NOT PREHEAT OVEN.

*Lisa Patterson, of the **Oregon Journal,**
who has "covered" our parties, sent me this
recipe. They are wonderful anytime, but especially with strawberries and ice cream.*

SOCIETY LEMON BARS

½ cup margarine
1 cup powdered sugar
1 cup flour

Mix and spread out (batter is stiff) in 9-inch square
pan. Bake 15 minutes at 350°, until pale tan, or paler.
Cool.

Mix:
2 tablespoons lemon juice
Rind of 1 lemon
2 eggs, well beaten
1 cup sugar
½ teaspoon baking powder
2 tablespoons flour

Pour over cooled crust and bake at 350° for 25 minutes.

Desserts

The finale to any meal

or

A simple way to entertain a larger number of guests who still want to sit down and visit.

Ardell Slentz has sent me many, many good recipes over the years. This pudding and sauce recipe is very good. The sauce can be used over a plain cake, too.

APPLE PUDDING

1 cup sugar
¼ cup shortening
1 egg
2 ½ cups chopped apples
1 teaspoon soda, sprinkled on apples
1 cup flour
¼ teaspoon salt
1 teaspoon each cinnamon and nutmeg

Cream shortening. Add sugar, egg, apples. Blend in dry ingredients. Pour into 8 x 8-inch pan. Bake at 350 to 375° for 40 minutes or until tests done.

Sauce:
1 cup Half and Half, or part condensed milk
½ cup margarine
1 cup sugar
1 teaspoon vanilla

Cook in double boiler 3 minutes. Thicken with 2 tablespoons cornstarch softened in water. Pour over cake before serving.

On a recent fact finding trip through the Middle East (not at government expense) Mark stopped in Turkey. He was entertained at The U.S. Embassy, where this dessert was served. He was so impressed with it that he asked for the recipe. It is light and tasty.

APPLE SOUFFLE

10 tart apples
6 egg whites
12 tablespoons powdered sugar
½ teaspoon cinnamon

Peel apples, cut into small pieces and cook with 2 tablespoons of powdered sugar until soft. Put this mixture through a sieve and add the cinnamon. Beat 6 egg whites with an electric beater for 1 minute. Then add the rest of the sugar and beat until the whites are thick and stand in peaks. Fold this into the apple mixture.
Oil a pyrex bowl and dust with a light coat of powdered sugar.

Bake at 400° for 15-20 minutes.

A not-too-fattening dessert!!

APRICOT SHERBET

½ cup water
1 ½ cups apricot nectar
2 tablespoons lemon juice
1 teaspoon gelatin
½ cup sugar
2 egg whites

Boil water and sugar for 5 minutes. Add dissolved gelatin and lemon juice. When cool, stir in apricot nectar. Pour into refrigerator tray and freeze. When partly frozen, place in chilled bowl and beat until frothy. Add two stiffly beaten egg whites. Blend until smooth. Return to refrigerator and freeze. Additional beating improves the texture.

Makes approximately 4 servings.

An even less fattening dessert.

APRICOT WHIP

Cover dried apricots with cold water and stew over a low flame until the fruit is soft, then sweeten to taste. Put the fruit through a food mill, or strain through a sieve, until you have 1 cup of pulp. Beat the whites of 2 eggs, slowly adding 2 tablespoons sugar after they begin to foam. When the whites are stiff, fold in the apricots. Chill in the refrigerator before serving.

Makes 4 servings.

The International Clubs in Washington were founded by the very charming and thoughtful Mrs. Ross Adair, whose husband is a Congressman from Indiana. Marian Adair, through her contacts with diplomatic wives (her husband is on the Foreign Relations Committee of the House), recognized a need for diplomatic, congressional and local wives to meet on a more informal basis.

I was invited to join International Club III. While our membership is perhaps the smallest of all the clubs, it is big on lasting international friendships. Trudy Robison (wife of Congressman Howard Robison of New York state) served this dessert at the first meeting I attended of International Club III. Every meeting since has been a sweet experience.

BLITZEN TORTE

½ cup butter
½ cup sugar
4 egg yolks
4 tablespoons milk
½ cup flour
1 teaspoon baking powder, mixed with 2 tablespoons flour

Beat 8 minutes until light and fluffy. Spread into two cake pans (8 or 9-inch round).

4 egg whites
1 cup sugar

Beat together until stiff. Spread meringue on top of the above mixture. Cover one meringue with chopped nuts. Bake in moderate oven for 25 minutes.

Turn out one layer on cake dish upside down (meringue on bottom), spread with strawberry jam. Whip ½ pint cream and spread over jam. Put second layer with nuts on top.

Best if not refrigerated before serving.

In blueberry season, you can use fresh blueberries for this recipe.

BLUEBERRY DESSERT

20 graham crackers
½ cup sugar
½ cup soft butter or margarine
8-ounce package cream cheese, softened
2 eggs
1 teaspoon vanilla
1 cup sugar
1 can blueberry pie filling
1 tablespoon lemon juice

Crush crackers (1 ½ cups). Mix with ½ cup sugar and butter. Pack on bottom of 9 x 13-inch pan. With mixer beat cheese, add eggs, vanilla and 1 cup sugar. Beat until fluffy. Spread over crackers and bake at 375° for 20 minutes. Cool. Combine pie filling (or 2 cups blueberries with juice, 2 tablespoons flour and 1 teaspoon cornstarch) with lemon juice. Heat to simmering. Cool. Spread over cheese mixture. Cool and chill well.

Serves 12 to 15.

A last minute dessert.

CANDIED BANANAS FROM THE ADOBE, YACHATS, OREGON

2-3 tablespoons butter
4 bananas, peeled and cut in half, lengthwise

Melt butter in heavy, cast iron skillet over low to medium heat. Lay bananas in skillet, cut side down. Cook until slightly browned. Sprinkle 2-3 tablespoons of sugar over bananas. Remove bananas from pan. Let sugar carmelize. Serve warm with sweetened whipped cream.

Next to diamonds, a girl's best friend is her hairdresser. On trips to Portland, Arden Eby has always adjusted to our busy schedule and managed to "squeeze me in" between and before appointments on his regular bookings. His wife, Carol, gave me this recipe, which is as creative as some of Arden's hairdos . . . I appreciate both of their talents.

CRANBERRY DESSERT

1 cup sugar
4 tablespoons melted butter
1 cup milk
2 cups cake flour
4 level teaspoons baking powder
2 cups whole, washed cranberries

Mix dry ingredients, then add milk and butter, then cranberries. Beat like waffle batter. Bake in square pan at 400° for 30 minutes.

Sauce:
1 ½ cups brown sugar
3 tablespoons flour
1 teaspoon vanilla
1 stick butter
⅔ cup white sugar
2 scant cups water

Serve sauce warm over cake. Cake may be served warm or cold. Makes a pretty holiday dessert.

FORGOTTEN CAKE

12 egg whites
½ teaspoon salt
1 teaspoon cream of tartar
2 cups sugar
1 teaspoon vanilla

Beat egg whites to soft peaks. Then add sugar gradually. Keep beating until very stiff. Add vanilla.
Put mixture into three 9-inch pie pans, lining as for a pie shell. Place in a preheated 450° oven, and turn off immediately. Leave overnight, or at least 4-5 hours. Do not open oven door. Put whipped cream between layers and decorate with sliced or whole strawberries on top of whipped cream. It's best if assembled in the morning and served for dinner that same day.

FUDGE TORTE A LA MODE

4 ounces unsweetened chocolate
1 cup (½ pound) butter or margarine
4 eggs
2 cups sugar
2 teaspoons vanilla
1 cup unsifted regular all-purpose flour
⅛ teaspoon salt
1 cup chopped Macadamia nuts or walnuts
1 package (10 ounces) frozen raspberries
Vanilla ice cream
Chocolate curls

Melt chocolate and butter in the top of a double boiler over simmering water. Set aside to cool.

Beat eggs until thick and lemon colored and gradually beat in sugar, 1 tablespoon at a time, beating until very thick. Beat in vanilla, mix in the melted chocolate and butter mixture and the flour and salt, mixing just until blended. Fold in chopped nuts. Turn into two buttered 9-inch pie pans. Bake at 325° for 30 to 35 minutes, or until top springs back when touched lightly. Cool. Pour sauce over it before serving.

Sauce:
Puree thawed raspberries and syrup in blender, then push through wire strainer. Top with ice cream.

May be packaged and frozen if desired (without sauce and ice cream).

A good "for a crowd" dessert.

LEMON DESSERT

2 envelopes unflavored gelatin
½ cup water
6 eggs, separated
½ cup sugar
½ cup scalded milk
¾ cup lemon juice
1 tablespoon grated lemon peel
½ cup sugar
½ cup chopped pecans
1 cup heavy cream, whipped
½ angel food cake (homemade preferred)
1 cup heavy cream, whipped
2 tablespoons sugar
¼ cup chopped pecans
Grated rind of one lemon

Soften gelatin in cold water. Beat egg yolks, combine
with ½ cup sugar and milk. Cook over boiling water
until thickened. Stir in softened gelatin until dissolved.
Cool and add first quantities of lemon juice and rind.
Beat egg whites until stiff, adding ½ cup sugar gradually while beating. Fold beaten egg whites, pecans
and 1 cup cream, whipped, into custard mixture. Alternate this mixture with strips of angel food cake in
a 3-quart mold. Chill several hours or overnight. Unmold. Add the 2 tablespoons sugar to second measure
of cream, whipped. Frost dessert with the whipped
cream and sprinkle with lemon rind and ¼ cup
chopped nuts.

I add 1 teaspoon of vanilla to this most delicious of all chocolate sauces.

MARY JANE DELLENBACK'S CHOCOLATE FUDGE SAUCE

½ cup butter
4 squares unsweetened chocolate
3 cups sugar
½ teaspoon salt
1 can (14 ounces) evaporated milk

In top of double boiler, over hot water, melt butter. Add chocolate and melt. Add sugar, 4 tablespoons at a time. Be sure sugar is moistened after each addition. The sauce becomes very thick and dry. Add salt. Stir in evaporated milk, a little at a time. (Add 1 teaspoon vanilla.) Serve hot. Makes 1 quart. Keep in refrigerator and reheat over hot water.

From Cassieta Walker comes this do-ahead dessert.

MOCHA DESSERT

½ can, or package, thin chocolate wafers, crushed
12 ounces marshmallows
1 cup strong coffee (5 teaspoons instant to 1 cup water)
1 pint whipping cream
1 cup pecans
1 teaspoon vanilla

Melt marshmallows and coffee in double boiler. Cool. Spread half the crushed wafers in bottom of buttered (lightly) dish or pan. Fold whipped cream in the coffee and marshmallow mix. Spread over wafers. Top with additional wafers and chill. Keeps well in refrigerator overnight.

The best thing about these recipes is the little special cups to serve them in. Any demitasse will do, however, and it does look elegant.

Try them both and see which you like best. Maxyne Davis is an "Ikebana" friend, and everything she presents looks like a delicate Japanese flower arrangement.

MAXYNE'S CHOCOLATE POT DE CREME

3 ounces German sweet chocolate
1 square bitter chocolate
6 eggs
1 pint cream
½ pinch salt
1 teaspoon vanilla

Desserts

Bring cream to a boil, stir in chocolates until melted. Cool mixture, beat in eggs, salt and vanilla and pour into six serving cups and chill.

Makes 6 servings.

MAXYNE'S POT DE CREME

1 small package (6 ounces) chocolate morsels
¾ cup milk, scalded
2 tablespoons sugar
Pinch of salt
1 teaspoon vanilla
1 egg

Put all ingredients, but milk, in blender; blend one minute. Pour over scalded milk; blend and pour into containers.

Makes 4 generous servings.
Takes 5 minutes to make.

SWEDISH NUT TORTE

4 egg yolks
¾ cup granulated sugar
1 ½ cup finely ground walnuts (or pecans) firmly packed
½ teaspoon packaged dry bread crumbs
½ teaspoon double acting baking powder
4 egg whites
18-20 small English Ivy leaves
1 tablespoon butter
¼ cup powdered sugar

Start heating oven to 375°. Grease, then line with wax paper, bottom of 9-inch layer cake pan. In small electric mixer bowl, with mixer at high speed, beat egg yolks with sugar until light and fluffy. With rubber spatula, fold in ground nuts, bread crumbs, baking powder, then egg, stiffly beaten. Pour into layer cake pan. Bake 25 to 30 minutes or until torte springs back when touched lightly in center. Cool in pan and remove to wire rack. Meanwhile, wash and dry ivy leaves. In small pan, over hot water, melt chocolate, add butter, stir until melted, remove from heat but leave over hot water. Now, with small spatula, spread thin layer of chocolate mixture on back of one of ivy leaves. Set leaf, chocolate side up, on waxed paper. Repeat with rest of leaves. Refrigerate until dry and set. Then remove, one by one, from refrigerator and carefully separate each chocolate leaf from green leaf by inserting small knife along edge, starting from stem end. Refrigerate right side up. Now, set torte bottom side up on cake plate. Sift confectioners' sugar over top. Then, with cake decorator and tube No. 3, filled with mocha cream, make a scalloped border around top of torte. Then arrange chocolate leaves, right side up, in border on top of mocha cream. Refrigerate. Cut in wedges to serve. Makes 8 or more servings.

Mocha Cream:
In small electric mixer bowl, with mixer at medium speed, mix 3 tablespoons butter with ¼ cup powdered sugar until light and fluffy. Now add ¾ cup powdered sugar, 2 tablespoons light cream, 3 tablespoons cocoa, 2 tablespoon instant coffee and 1 teaspoon vanilla. Beat until very smooth.
Makes 1 cup.

*Real Swiss chocolate is a must for this recipe.
The recipe comes from Madame Schnyder,
wife of the Ambassador from Switzerland.*

SWISS CHOCOLATE CREAM

13 ½-ounce bar unsweetened Swiss chocolate
2 eggs
Sugar to taste
1 cup cream, whipped

Melt chocolate with a little hot water in double boiler. Add sugar to taste. Beat eggs lightly. Take melted chocolate from heat and mix gently with eggs. Let cool a little and fold in the whipped cream. Chill.

Serves 3-4 persons.

*Don't forget the 2 cups of water, like I did the
first time I made this pudding. Dry chocolate
is really very bitter!*

AUNT JANET'S OLD TENNESSEE PUDDING

Mix in a 13 x 9 x 2-inch pan:
1 cup brown sugar
½ cup cocoa
2 cups water
Add 50 or more miniature marshmallows (2 BIG handfuls). Mix 1 package devils food cake according to directions on package. Drop by spoonfuls on top of mixture in the pan. Sprinkle marshmallows and 1 cup chopped nuts over top. Bake 45 minutes at 350°. Serve warm with whipped cream.

Entrees

*The Entree section of this book has ex-
panded some over the last one. Once you
have decided on the main course, it's
easier to build the rest of your menu.
Someday I hope to do a menu cookbook.*

The brunch we had during the weekend of President Nixon's Inauguration featured this Baked Corned Beef. Do be sure to get a brisket of beef that says "for oven roasting" on the label.

BAKED CORNED BEEF

3 ½ pound corned beef for oven baking
Cloves
Pineapple Rings
Brown sugar
1 teaspoon dry mustard

Bake the corned beef at 325° about 2 hours. Remove from oven and stud with cloves; decorate with pineapple slices; sprinkle with brown sugar mixed with a little pineapple juice and a teaspoon of dry mustard. Return to oven for 30-45 minutes, until browned. Let stand 15 minutes before slicing.

Another of Aunt Dorothy's recipes —

BARBECUED BEEF BRISKET

5 pounds of brisket
Rub with salt and pepper
1 clove garlic, cut up
5 or more drops liquid smoke
Enough water to cover meat
1 bottle of your favorite barbecue sauce

Boil all but barbecue sauce in "water to cover" for 3 hours, covered. Strain and save ½ liquid stock. Chill meat, preferably overnight, to make it congeal. Slice next day and place in deep rectangular pan, or large loaf pan. Pour your favorite bottled barbecue sauce over top and smear between slices. Pour some of liquid stock around meat. Cover with foil and bake at 300° for 1 hour.

This is a great recipe to do ahead and freeze. Bring it out for unexpected guests — especially if they are the "young crowd."

Iris Collins said she kept one in the freezer throughout all of her daughter, Coni's, high school and college years — hairstyles may change, but appetites don't seem to.

BEEF ON SOUR DOUGH

1 round loaf Sour Dough French Bread (8 inches in diameter)
1 large onion, coarsely chopped
2 tablespoons salad oil
1 can (6 ounces) tomato paste
1 small can (2 ¼ ounces) sliced, ripe olives, drained
1 can (2 ounces) sliced mushrooms, drained
1 teaspoon basil
¾ teaspoon salt
¼ teaspoon pepper
1 pound ground beef
1 egg, slightly beaten
Soft butter
2 slices jack cheese, cut in triangles

Cut thin slice ½-inch deep from top of French bread, scoop out most of bread; tear into small pieces to get 1 ½ cups. Brown onion in oil; combine with rest of ingredients; spoon into hollow bread shell. Lightly butter outside of loaf with soft butter. Wrap tightly in foil. Bake in 350° oven for 1 hour and 15 minutes. Remove foil and arrange cheese triangles over top. Return to oven for 3 minutes. Slice to serve like pie.

Makes 6 to 8 servings.

If everyone in political life had supporters like Elsie Isaacson Eyre, life would be sweet. She's one of those rare individuals who has supported us through thick and thin since that first campaign for the governorship when she was on our Coos County Committee. Although Elsie is no longer a constituent, she continues to give us moral support and, like those good shots to a golfer, she keeps us going. Here is one of her favorite recipes — Chicken Divan with Cheese Sauce.

CHICKEN DIVAN WITH CHEESE SAUCE

4 boxes frozen broccoli spears
5-6 full chicken breasts

Place chicken breasts in water. Bring to a boil and immediately turn to simmer. Cook until tender, about 1 hour. Cool chicken. Remove from bones and slice. Cook broccoli until almost tender — about 3 minutes less than instructions. Place broccoli in baking dish 9 x 15 inches. Top with chicken slices; cover with cheese sauce; sprinkle with paprika and bake in 325° oven for about 40 minutes.

Cheese Sauce:
Melt 4 tablespoons butter in saucepan. Blend in 2 tablespoons flour. Stir in slowly 3 cups milk. When sauce is smooth and boiling, reduce heat and add 2 cups processed cheese (diced). Season with 1 teaspoon salt, ¼ teaspoon paprika and few grains cayenne and 1 teaspoon dry mustard (optional). Stir sauce until cheese is melted. Makes 4 cups.

Makes 8 servings of Chicken Divan.

Carol Gessford of Coos Bay was named
*Homemaker of the Year for 1969 by **Family***
***Circle Magazine.** We entertained Carol*
at a luncheon here in Washington and sub-
sequently I wrote an article for the magazine.
I asked Carol for a recipe which I might
use in this book. Her recipe for chicken
is not only easy but was an instant success
with my family. Carol says, "You can start
this as you run out the door and finish after
a full day of busy activities. It will look
like you have cooked all day." AGREED!
I served it with boiled rice and peaches and
a tossed salad with oil and vinegar dressing.

It is really an honor for the State of Oregon
to have one of its citizens be so recognized.

CAROL GESSFORD'S
CHICKEN IN SOY SAUCE

Marinate chicken parts in 1 part salad oil and 2 parts
soy sauce for 6 hours. Bake covered 45 minutes at
325°. Uncover and broil 2 to 3 minutes until brown.
Pass the juice from chicken when serving.

A good St. Patrick's Day recipe

CORNED BEEF CASSEROLE

1 package (8 ounces) broad noodles
1 can (12 ounces) diced corned beef
¼ pound American cheese, diced
1 can (10 ½ ounces) cream of chicken or cream of
mushroom soup
1 cup milk
½ cup chopped onion
¾ cup buttered crumbs

Cook noodles and drain. Add next five ingredients,
and pour into buttered casserole. Top with crumbs
and bake in moderate oven about 45 minutes.

This recipe has a slightly sweet flavor and is tasty.

CORN-TOPPED BEEF CASSEROLE

1 medium onion, minced
2 tablespoons shortening
2 pounds ground beef
2 tablespoons flour
2-3 tablespoons chili powder
3 teaspoons salt
¼ teaspoon pepper
½ cup sliced carrots
¼ cup brown sugar
1 can (17 ounces) cream-style corn
2 eggs, well beaten
3 tablespoons sugar
1 cup milk

Cook onion in shortening 2-3 minutes. Add beef and cook until meat loses its red color. Mix flour, chili powder, 2 teaspoons salt and the pepper with ½ cup water and stir into mixture. Cook, stirring, until thickened. Remove from heat and fold in carrots and brown sugar. Put in a 3-quart casserole about 3 inches deep. Mix corn, remaining salt, raw eggs, 2 tablespoons sugar and milk. Cook over medium heat, stirring, until thickened. Pour over mixture in casserole and sprinkle with 1 tablespoon sugar. Bake in moderate oven (350°) 30 to 40 minutes.

Makes 6-8 servings.

Janine Driss, whose husband was Ambassador from Tunisia, and President of the International Club to which I belong, gave me this recipe. It's wonderful, though complicated.

COUSCOUS

1-pound package of "couscous"
6 pieces of chicken or lamb
1 pound carrots
2 or 3 small turnips
3 potatoes
2 teaspoons Italian tomato sauce
¼ cup olive oil
Onion, salt, pepper and pimiento powder to taste

Wet the couscous 30 minutes before cooking by pouring a little bit of water on it, so that it is wet but not soaked. Put oil in pan over moderate heat. Add chopped onion, then the meat. Saute until both are brown. Add pimiento, tomato sauce, salt, pepper, and simmer for 15 minutes. Then add 2 quarts of cold water and put in the vegetables, except the potatoes, which will be added at the last moment; then put the wet couscous in the top part of the pan, the potatoes in the bottom part, cover and cook for half an hour. Remove from heat, put the couscous in a vegetable dish, wetting it with part of the liquid from the vegetables and put around vegetables and meat.

Dolly Saxbe's husband came to the Senate in the 91st Congress. Both have contributed a great deal to life "on the Hill." Besides being a good cook, Dolly is a good artist.

DOLLY SAXBE'S
RAGOUT OF BEEF WITH WALNUTS

3 pounds lean beef (cubed)
3 tablespoons shortening
18 small onions
5 tablespoons cornstarch
¾ cup cooking sherry
¼ teaspoon thyme
4 sprigs parsley
2 tablespoons finely-shredded orange rind
2 bay leaves
1 clove garlic
2 ½ cups beef or chicken stock
1 ½ tablespoons salt
½ teaspoon pepper
¾ cup walnut halves (Oregon English)
3 cups thinly diced celery

Cube beef; brown in shortening and *remove*. Brown onion and add everything except walnuts, celery and orange rind. Cook to boiling point and simmer 4 hours *at least*. Add walnuts, celery and orange rind. Thicken with 5 tablespoons cornstarch in ½ cup water. Serve with rice or noodles.

Can be frozen to save for "drop in" guests.

We like this for Sunday lunch.

DOUBLE CHEESE SOUFFLE

⅓ cup butter or margarine
⅓ cup flour
½ teaspoon salt
⅛ teaspoon pepper
⅛ teaspoon ground nutmeg
1 ½ cups milk
6 egg yolks, well beaten
¾ cup shredded Swiss cheese
¾ cup grated Parmesan cheese
6 egg whites
¼ teaspoon cream of tartar
2 tablespoons grated Parmesan cheese

Melt butter or margarine in saucepan; stir in flour, salt, pepper and nutmeg. Cook over medium heat, stirring constantly, until mixture bubbles. Remove from heat; stir in milk, slowly. Cook over medium heat, stirring constantly, until mixture thickens and bubbles (sauce will be quite thick). Remove from heat; beat mixture slowly into egg yolks. Beat in Swiss cheese and ¾ cup Parmesan cheese. (Souffle can be made ahead to this point.) Heat oven to 350°. Beat egg whites and cream of tartar in large bowl until stiff, but not dry. Fold cheese sauce gently into egg whites. Turn into ungreased 2-quart souffle dish, or 8 individual souffle dishes. Sprinkle with 2 tablespoons Parmesan cheese. Bake large souffle 45 to 50 minutes, individual souffles 25 to 30 minutes or until puffed and fairly firm to the touch. Serve with Tomato Mushroom Sauce. Makes 8 servings.

TOMATO MUSHROOM SAUCE

Saute ½ pound sliced mushrooms in ¼ cup butter or margarine for 5 minutes; remove and reserve. Add 2 tablespoons butter or margarine to pan. Blend in 2 tablespoons flour, 2 teaspoons sugar, ¼ teaspoon salt, and ½ teaspoon leaf basil, crumbled. Cook, stirring constantly, until bubbly. Stir in 1 can (18 ounces) tomato juice, slowly. Cook over medium heat, stirring constantly, to boiling. Add mushrooms and 3 tablespoons chopped parsley; heat through. Makes about 2 ½ cups sauce.

Good Neighbor Chicken is elegant and simple to make. I usually keep a pan ready to go in the freezer and have used it to take to friends who were ill and couldn't cook for their families. I serve it with Petite Peas, boiled rice and a fruit salad. "Aunt Janet's Tennessee Pudding" makes a good dessert.

This is a favorite recipe of Frankie Welch, of Virginia, who, besides running a successful boutique, has designed several winning political scarves.

GOOD NEIGHBOR CHICKEN

8 chicken breasts, boned and cut in half
16 slices bacon
½ pound dried chipped beef or ham
2 cans cream of chicken soup
½ soup can cooking sherry
½ to 1 teaspoon curry

Cut chipped beef or ham in small pieces and scatter in bottom of greased casserole. Wrap a slice of bacon around each piece of chicken. Secure with toothpick. Place on chipped beef. Cover completely with soup and sherry mixture and bake uncovered in 300° oven for 2 ½ to 3 hours.

Serve this with canned peaches (with the centers filled with cranberry sauce), French cut string beans, and Florida Citrus Cake for dessert.

IRIS COLLINS' BAKED CHICKEN LOAF

Combine:
4 cups finely diced cooked chicken (put through food chopper)
2 cups chicken broth
3 eggs
1 ½ cups soft bread crumbs
1 ½ teaspoons salt
¼ teaspoon paprika
1 teaspoon Worcestershire sauce
½ cup minced celery
¼ teaspoon curry
⅛ teaspoon beau monde seasoning
1 onion, put through chopper
1 ½ tablespoons lemon juice

Mix all ingredients and put into buttered casserole. Set in pan of hot water and cook about 1 ½ hours, until knife comes out clean, at 350°. Let stand 10 minutes before unmolding. Serve with mushroom sauce.

Mushroom Sauce:
Mix 1 can mushroom or cream of chicken soup with 1 can mushrooms and liquid. Heat.

*From Mrs. 99 to Mrs. 100 — Joy and Howard
Baker came to the Senate when we did.
Mark was No. 100 and Howard was No. 99.
Joy and I always enjoyed these two dis-
tinctive numbers in the order of Senate
seniority.*

JOY'S BAKED CHICKEN

Melt 1 cube butter in a casserole dish. Roll 8 pieces
of chicken in this melted butter and bake at 400°,
turning frequently, for 45 minutes. Meanwhile, mix:
1 cup sour cream
1 can cream of mushroom soup
1 to 2 teaspoons Worcestershire sauce
Salt and pepper to taste

Pour this mixture over chicken. Reduce heat in oven
to 325° and bake an additional 15 minutes.

Serve with a mixture of long grain and wild rice,
peas and onions and a Tomato Aspic.

Katie Malone is a faithful member of the Ladies of the Senate Red Cross group and hers was the first smiling face to greet and welcome me in January of 1967. Her heart is as warm as her cooking.

KATIE MALONE'S TAMALE CASSEROLE

1 turkey (10-12 pounds), stewed until tender
3 cans niblet corn, drained
3 small cans, or 1 large and 1 small can, pitted ripe olives, drained
2 small cans mushrooms (stems and bits) — do not use fresh mushrooms
½ pint heavy cream
2 regular tamales per person (not green corn tamales)
4 cups clear, thin enchilada sauce
1 cup cracker crumbs
Paprika to taste
Grated Longhorn cheese with ⅛ cup grated sharp cheddar

Cut turkey from bones into large pieces. Add corn, olives, mushrooms and tamales which have been broken into bite-size pieces. Add cream and enchilada sauce (perhaps not quite all). Mix with hands. Mixture will feel too moist. Smooth mixture in a thick layer in large baking dish. Cover generously with grated cheese, cracker crumbs and paprika. Bake at 350° for 40 to 50 minutes. Serve with Helepenas, Kosher salt and cracked red and black pepper.

Makes 12 servings.

One of Lois Oberdorf's guaranteed good buffet dishes . . .

CHICKEN AND MUSHROOM CASSEROLE

36 pieces chicken
Salt, pepper and paprika
¾ cup butter or margarine
¾ pound fresh mushrooms, sliced
¼ cup flour
1 ½ cups chicken broth
6 tablespoons cooking sherry
3 sprigs fresh rosemary or
½ teaspoon crumbled dried rosemary

Sprinkle chicken pieces with salt, pepper and paprika. Brown in half the butter and remove to casserole or shallow baking dish. Add remaining butter to drippings and saute sliced mushrooms until tender. Sprinkle flour over mushrooms and stir in chicken broth, sherry and rosemary. Cook until thickened, then pour over chicken. Cover and bake in a 350° oven for 45 minutes. If casserole has been refrigerated, bake 1 hour.

Serves 18.

Another recipe from Marian Lowry Fischer.

MARIAN'S SIMPLE CHICKEN

Lightly grease a baking dish and spread a cup of uncooked, regular rice (not precooked rice) over bottom of pan. Shake an envelope of dry onion soup mix over rice. Dilute 1 can cream of mushroom soup with 1 can water and blend well; pour over rice and onion soup. Place chicken pieces over top and bake 1 ½ hours at 350°.

"Cousin Mary" says this is a really good main dish, that is even popular with her children.

MARY McCLUER'S NEW MEXICAN CHILI

1 ½ pounds round steak
¼ cup chili powder
2 cups bouillon or beef broth
1 teaspoon salt
1 teaspoon oregano
1 tablespoon vinegar
1 clove garlic, minced
1 small onion, diced

Cut meat into ½-inch cubes or have meat ground on grinder fitted with a chili plate. Place meat in large skillet with chili powder, bouillon, salt, oregano, vinegar, garlic and onion. Cover and simmer over low heat until meat is tender and mixture thick and saucy in consistency. (About 45 minutes to 1 hour). Sprinkle with chopped raw onion and serve hot in deep bowls, with tortillas as an accompaniment, or serve on plates with refried beans, on hamburgers, sliced pot roast or omelet, or spoon over fried eggs on hot tortillas. Makes 4 to 6 servings.

Here is a recipe I picked up in Pebble Beach a number of years back from Elizabeth Alward. She is a friend of Aunt Dorothy's. While I haven't used it for a long time, I'm glad I ran across it again. It is delicious.

MARY'S TOWERS

Toast 1 slice of bread for each person. Preheat oven to 350°. Flavor ground beef your favorite way (Worcestershire and salt). Place the ground beef all over one side of the toast, very thickly (at least 1 ¼ inches). Place on that a slice of onion, then a slice of salted, peeled tomato, then a slice of cheddar cheese. Put all the towers into a low baking pan and place in oven. Bake for 30 minutes. No need to look at it. In 30 minutes it will be delicious.

These towers and a tossed green salad and maybe a dessert make a satisfying meal.

Marian gave her son, Michael, credit for this recipe. It makes any cut of meat tastier, but for nights that "the boss comes to dinner" sirloin steak is the order of the day.

MICHAEL BURROS' BARBECUE STEAK SAUCE

4 pounds sirloin steak
Salt with 1 tablespoon Kosher salt and dip in ½ cup
olive oil before marinating in the following:
2 tablespoons butter
1 clove garlic, crushed
Juice of ½ lemon
½ cup tomato paste
½ cup Worcestershire sauce
Freshly ground pepper
1 tablespoon soy sauce

Heat above ingredients until bubbling. Marinate
steak about 2 hours in sauce. Sear marinated steak
quickly over hot coals. Baste steak with sauce each
time it is turned. Should take ½ hour to 45 minutes
a side, depending on how rare you like your steak.

This recipe is a salute to the lamb industry in Oregon.

MINTED RACK OF LAMB

2 pound rack of lamb
Salt and pepper
½ cup mint jelly
¼ teaspoon cinnamon
¼ teaspoon cloves
1 can (1 pound) applesauce

Place lamb on rack in shallow roasting pan; sprinkle
with salt and pepper. Roast in 325° oven for 1 ½ hours.
Meanwhile, combine jelly, cinnamon and cloves in a
saucepan; bring to a boil and stir until jelly melts.
Stir ¼ cup of jelly mixture into applesauce; chill.
Drain off lamb drippings; heat remaining mint glaze
and brush over lamb. Roast 30 minutes longer, or
until meat thermometer registers 175-180°, depending
upon desired degree of doneness. Serve lamb with
minted applesauce. Garnish with mandarin oranges
and pears, if desired.

It was always fun to go to Dorothy Dougan's house on those college weekends home. Specialty of the house was her mother's "South American Turkey." Mr. Dougan encouraged his wife to serve this dish because, he said, "after all, your guests don't come here that often that they would tire of it." This seems to be a wise philosophy for anyone who has one dish that she does extremely well, and which is greatly enjoyed by her guests.

MRS. DOUGAN'S SOUTH AMERICAN TURKEY

1 turkey (15 pounds)
1 self-basting roasting pan
1 lemon
2 ½ sticks cinnamon
2 bay leaves
5 dashes angustura bitters
½-1 cup cooking sherry
½ teaspoon poultry seasoning
1 cup pitted black olives
1 cup blanched almonds
Enough of your favorite dressing to stuff turkey

Stuff turkey your usual way. Slice lemon in thin slices. Put ½ the slices on bottom of roasting pan and ½ on top of the turkey. Combine cooking sherry, bitters, bay leaves, cinnamon, olives, poultry seasoning. Pour over turkey and bake 20 minutes per pound at 325°. Remove turkey to deep platter and pour juices over the turkey. Sprinkle almonds over the turkey. With each slice of the turkey, serve some dressing and some of the gravy.

Some time ago I watched a cooking television show which featured an interview with Senator and Mrs. McGovern of South Dakota. I later checked with Mrs. McGovern about the ingredients. She said they were correct, except that she used good, old-fashioned mid-western vegetables.

MRS. GEORGE McGOVERN'S FAMILY STYLE STEW

Finely chop 2 medium-sized onions. Brown in 2 tablespoons of oil, along with 2 pounds bite-sized stewing beef. Season with:
1 tablespoon salt
½ teaspoon fresh ground pepper
1 tablespoon flour

Pour in 1 ½ cups water. To this add:
Peas
Potatoes
Carrots

Pour into a covered casserole and bake for 2 ½ -3 hours at 200°.

You may add parsley, garlic, Parmesan cheese and basil before serving.

Mrs. George Maurice Morris is a true gentle woman, charming hostess, and an authority on 18th Century American Furniture, and her home is full of priceless antiques. She serves authentic early American menus at before-concert dinners, a favorite way of entertaining. One evening she served turkey with a **Sweet Herb Dressing** *and* **Pilaf of Rice with Pignola and Pistachio Nuts.** *Mrs. Morris was generous enough to share her recipes and I hope they taste as good in your house as they did in hers.*

On nights when you serve these recipes, it is a special touch to have "dinner by candlelight" as they did in colonial America.

SWEET HERB DRESSING

Cook giblets of birds or turkey in 2 cups of water.
1 package commercial stuffing mix
1 medium-sized onion, grated
2 stalks celery, grated
¼ pound butter or margarine
2 teaspoons marjoram
¼ teaspoon of sage or poultry seasoning
Grate all liver

Mix butter or margarine with 1 cup of broth from giblets. Add stuffing, liver, onion, and celery. Mix well. Add seasoning and rest of giblet broth if needed. Salt to taste.

PILAF OF RICE WITH PIGNOLA AND PISTACHIO NUTS

2 cups cooked rice
¼ cup pignola nuts
¼ cup blanched pistachio nuts (not salted)
3 tablespoons butter
1 to 2 teaspoons mace

Place butter in heavy iron frying pan over low heat. Add pignola nuts and lightly shake until the color of a popcorn kernel. Add rice. Lift in pistachio nuts. Sprinkle mace to taste and cook until rice is heated.

Makes 6-8 servings.

*Over the years we have celebrated New
Year's Eve quietly at home with just one or
two other people. One year I served Welsh
Rarebit which is a favorite dish of Mark's.
This was one of those "improvise on a
theme" recipes, and when both he and Carl
Collins said it was the best, I decided to
include it as "New Year's Eve Welsh Rarebit."*

NEW YEAR'S EVE WELSH RAREBIT

Cut into small pieces 3 ½ cups of an Oregon cheddar
cheese

2 tablespoons butter
1 ½ cups stale ale (open can at least 3 hours before
using)
½ cup cream
½ teaspoon dry mustard
½ teaspoon paprika
3 egg yolks

In top of double boiler, melt first 2 ingredients. Add
remaining ingredients, one at a time. Pour into chafing dish. Serve over toasted french bread and with a
tossed salad.

When I first came to Washington, the hostess for the first two luncheons I attended served Quiche Lorraine and a tossed salad. I know now that it is the "in" menu.

If you put the bacon on a broiling pan for about 30 minutes at 300°, this is not such a hard dish to prepare. It can be done the day before and heated through the day you are to serve it. You can also use this filling in small tart-size crusts for an appetizer.

QUICHE LORRAINE

Pastry for 10-inch pie shell or quiche dish

1 pound cooked bacon, crumbled
6 eggs
2 tablespoons flour
½ teaspoon nutmeg
3 cups light cream
3 tablespoons melted butter
3 cups freshly grated Swiss cheese

Line pie pan or quiche dish with pastry; crumble ½ the bacon on top of pastry. Blend eggs, flour, nutmeg and cream and butter in blender at high speed for 1 minute. Pour over bacon. Sprinkle cheese over this and then sprinkle final layer of bacon. Bake for 40-45 minutes or until a knife inserted in center comes out clean.

This recipe will serve six generously.

This is one of the children's very favorite of Mother's recipes . . .

SPECIAL SLOPPY JOES

1-2 tablespoons olive oil
2 pounds ground chuck
1 medium onion, finely chopped
Juice of ½ lemon, plus ½ of rind
Juice of 1 orange, plus ½ of rind
2 tablespoons sugar (or more to taste)
1 teaspoon salt
¼ teaspoon nutmeg
¼ - ½ teaspoon cinnamon
1 teaspoon chili powder
1 bay leaf
¼ teaspoon celery salt
½ teaspoon garlic powder (optional)

Brown ground beef in olive oil. Add onion, lemon juice and ½ of rind, orange juice and ½ of rind, and all remaining ingredients. Stir and simmer over low heat, covered for 1-1 ½ hours. Remove rinds. Spoon over heated hamburger buns.

Makes 8-10 servings.

Mr. Earl Zwingle requested this from the Maitre d'hotel, Coronado Country Club, El Paso, Texas . . . Earl is a milinery man; and besides knowing good recipes, he knows the latest silhouettes for hats each season.

STEAK CARNE ASADA

Broil steak with green chili pepper strips, either fresh or canned chili strips may be used. Salt and pepper to taste.

Mary Aiken, one of my college roommates who was on an educational leave of absence from IBM to work for Mark in Washington, brought all of the ingredients for this recipe over one night and assembled it before you could say "IBM!" The result is delicious.

TURKEY TETRAZZINI

2 cups sliced mushrooms
6 tablespoons butter
4 tablespoons flour
3 cups light cream
2 cups diced, cooked turkey
1 teaspoon salt
½ teaspoon celery salt
Dash pepper
1 cup cooked thin spaghetti, cut into 1-inch pieces
½ cup Parmesan cheese

Saute mushrooms in butter until tender. Add flour and stir until smooth. Add cream and cook until thickened, stirring constantly. Add turkey, salt, pepper, celery salt and spaghetti; heat thoroughly. Turn into greased shallow baking dish or eight individual ramekins. Sprinkle generously with Parmesan cheese. Place under broiler until browned. Serve at once.

Makes 8 servings.

Jacqueline Hirsh taught French to President John Kennedy and Caroline. She has also taught me a few phrases. What is even more important than the French was her kindness in bringing this dish for my family during an illness I had. She is indeed a good neighbor. Incidentally, history tells us that Marengo, and its way of cooking, was a favorite of Napoleon's.

VEAL MARENGO

1 ½ tablespoons butter
1 ½ tablespoons oil
2 pounds veal roast, cut in pieces
2 large onions
1 tablespoon flour (more may be needed)
1 clove garlic (minced)
1 cup cooking sherry (white)
1 cup water
1 or 2 tablespoons tomato paste (or ketchup)
Salt and pepper to taste
5 sprigs parsley
Thyme
¼ bay leaf
½ pound mushrooms
Chopped parsley
4 slices stale bread (crusts off)
Shortening

Heat butter and oil well and brown onions and then brown meat. When well browned, add flour and mix. Add garlic, stir in wine, water and tomato paste. Add salt and pepper and herbs in "bouquet garni" (parsley, thyme and bay leaf tied in cheese cloth). Cover and cook gently for 1 hour. Wash and stem mushrooms and add them to the veal. Continue cooking for another half hour, then remove bouquet garni. Make croutons out of stale bread and brown them slightly. Serve on a bed of rice, decorated with the croutons and very young, small early peas.

Cowboys and Indians are synonymous to the West in some people's minds. One of the delights of the days in the Governor's office was the opportunity to be close enough to participate in many Oregon festivals. At the Indian Arts Festival in La Grande, I became better acquainted with June Poitras (who lives in Portland). She sent me this "Indian Menu." I have not tested the venison recipe, because of lack of the main ingredient; but for you who have "hunters" in your family, I'd say it is worth a try.

VENISON AND MUSHROOMS

Trim meat from bone and cut in small pieces (even shoulder and tougher parts can be used). Dredge in seasoned flour and fry until brown. Use a lot of oil to brown meat, and then drain off excess oil to brown mushrooms. If canned mushrooms are used, include liquid; add water, if necessary, and steam for at least an hour. Serve with wild rice.

June says she serves this with green vegetables and olives and pickles and pine nuts; Huckleberry pie, or Wild Plum Jam and Hot Rolls; or Wild Plum Sundaes with soft vanilla ice cream.

Mrs. B. B. Hickenlooper was kind enough to send me this recipe. Verna sat immediately behind us when Mark was sworn into the United States Senate. Mark has known Senator Hickenlooper for many years and it is always sad to have a colleague retire. We wish for them many happy years.

VERNA HICKENLOOPER'S BELGIAN BEEF STEW

½ cup unsifted all-purpose flour
2 tablespoons salt
½ teaspoon pepper
2 pounds chuck, cut in 1-inch pieces
½ cup salad oil
2 pounds onions, peeled and sliced
1 clove garlic, crushed
1 ½ cups water
1 tablespoon soy sauce
1 tablespoon Worcestershire sauce
1 tablespoon bottled steak sauce
2 bay leaves
½ teaspoon dried thyme leaves
2 pounds potatoes, pared and quartered
1 package (10 ounces) frozen peas
2 tablespoons chopped parsley

Combine flour, salt and pepper; use to coat chuck cubes well. In ¼ cup hot oil (in Dutch oven or kettle), saute onion and garlic until onion is tender — 8-10 minutes. Remove and set aside. Heat remaining oil in Dutch oven. Add chuck and brown well on all sides. Add onion and garlic, along with water, soy sauce, thyme; mix well. Bring mixture to boil. Reduce heat; simmer covered 1 ½ hours. Add potatoes, simmer covered 20 minutes, or until potatoes are tender. Add peas, simmer covered 8 minutes longer or just until peas are tender. Place stew in serving dish and garnish with the chopped parsley.

Makes 6 servings.

Entrees

This recipe comes from Bob Ogle who, besides being a good cook, has one of the finest Indian artifacts collections in Oregon.

VILLAGE SPECIAL SWISS STEAK

2 pounds beef round, cut into 4 servings
1 cup flour
1 teaspoon paprika
3 tablespoons shortening
Salt and pepper to taste
1 medium onion, chopped
1 can (8 ounces) tomato soup
1 teaspoon monosodium glutamate
1 tablespoon catsup
1 garlic button, chopped
1 can (8 ounces) mushrooms, diced
1 ounce cooking sherry

Press steaks into combined flour and paprika, seasoned with salt and pepper to taste. Pound into meat. Braise steaks in melted shortening. When brown on both sides, add remaining ingredients and bake at 375° for 30 minutes.

Makes 4 servings.

This recipe came from Mrs. James Jensen, whose husband was president of Oregon State University. Chris Jensen was more fun to watch than the team players in the annual University of Oregon — Oregon State University football game. Their team won more than mine, and I think it was her enthusiastic rooting and her large, orange felt hat that did the trick.

VIVA LA CHICKEN CASSEROLE

4 cooked chicken breasts, whole
12 corn tortillas
1 can (10 ½ ounces) cream of chicken soup
1 can (10 ½ ounces) cream of mushroom soup
1 cup milk
1 onion, grated or minced
2 cans green chile salsa (sauce)
1 pound cheddar cheese, shredded

Bone chicken, cut in large pieces. Cut tortillas in 1-inch strips. Mix soups, milk, onion and chile salsa. Add 2 or 3 tablespoons water, or chicken bouillon. Grease large shallow casserole. Place half of tortillas on bottom, cover with half of chicken and ⅓ of sauce. Repeat using sauce last. Top with cheese. Refrigerate 24 hours. Bake at 300° for 1-1 ½ hours.

Makes 10-12 servings.

*This is that **one recipe** which will have all
your guests copying from, or buying, the
book. Meredith Grupe, who gave me the
recipe, was the teacher of the 3-year-old class
at Suburban Nursery School.*

WALNUT STUFFED CHICKEN BREASTS

4 small chicken breasts (boned)
Lemon juice
¾ cube of melted butter
3 cups toasted bread crumbs
⅓ cup chopped onion
2 teaspoons parsley flakes
¾ cup chopped walnuts
¾ teaspoon monosodium glutamate
Salt and pepper
½ cup chopped celery

Mix together toasted bread crumbs, ½ of melted
butter, onion, celery, parsley, walnuts and monosodium glutamate with enough water to moisten.
Make 4 mounds of stuffing and arrange on 4 squares
of double thickness aluminum foil. (Grease foil with
butter or margarine in very center of square first.)
Place on cookie sheet. Brush both sides of chicken
breasts with lemon juice, then remaining butter.
Sprinkle with salt and pepper. Place an open chicken
breast over each mound of stuffing. Fold the foil up
around the top of chicken to make individual package.
Bake 40 minutes at 350°, then open packages and
bake for additional 20 minutes at 400°.

Pickles & Relishes

There's not much to say for pickles, except that they do add an extra dimension to any meal. With apologies to the commercial brands — all — there is just nothing like the homemade ones.

Both of these are delicious with beef, ham, or pork chops.

APPLE CHUTNEY

1 can (20 ounces) apple slices
½ cup raisins
¾ cup molasses
½ cup vinegar
½ teaspoon salt
1 teaspoon ginger
1 teaspoon dry mustard
1 tablespoon curry powder

Combine all ingredients in saucepan. Bring to a boil, stirring occasionally. Reduce heat and simmer 15 minutes. Serve hot or cold as meat accompaniment.

FRUIT RELISH — FROM WHOM?

6 peaches
6 pears
6 onions
6 tomatoes
3 green peppers
4 cups vinegar
4 cups sugar
2 tablespoons salt
2 tablespoons pickling spice (in a bag)

All fruit is to be peeled and cut into small pieces (½ inch). Bring all ingredients to a boil in a large pot, simmer for 1 hour. Bottle while hot. Small jars make nice gifts.

Marian Burros, in her Sunday Food Column, said these could "be used as a condiment with meat, a dessert (light and refreshing) or at a brunch table where something more elaborate than a glass of orange juice is wanted." They are good and you choose the time you wish to serve them.

GINGERED LEMON ORANGES

6 medium oranges, peeled and sliced into ¼-inch cartwheels
¼ cup pecan halves
½ cup freshly squeezed orange juice
1 teaspoon freshly grated lemon peel
¼ cup freshly squeezed lemon juice
¼ cup light corn syrup
1 teaspoon chopped, candied ginger

Cut orange cartwheels into thirds or quarters; combine with pecans in heatproof glass bowl. Combine remaining ingredients in saucepan; boil for 5 minutes, stirring constantly. Pour hot syrup over orange pieces; cover and chill several hours until well chilled and flavors have mellowed. Will keep in refrigerator for a couple of days.

Makes 4 cups.

Dr. Charles Mills delivered all four of our children. His wife, Margaret, gave up several holidays while we all "waited." On one of these occasions she had us to dinner. She served this delicious fruit. I use it often with ham or chicken.

MARGARET MILLS' CURRIED FRUIT

Drain 2 large cans of salad fruit, or your own assortment of canned fruits. Place in shallow casserole and top with mixture of:

1 cup brown sugar
2 teaspoons curry powder
1 tablespoon flour (or corn starch)

Dot with butter and moisten with a little fruit juice. Bake 1 hour at 350°. Refrigerate for 48 hours. Reheat to serve.

For larger quantities it is less expensive to use 1 can each:

peaches, pears, apricots, pineapple, oranges, etc. Chunks of fresh bananas are good, too.

MAXINE NEEDHAM'S PICKLES

4 to 5 quarts young, thin cucumbers (cut ⅛-inch thick)
7 ⅓ cups cider vinegar
3 tablespoons non-iodized salt
4 to 6 cups sugar (experiment with less sugar)
1 tablespoon mustard seed
2 ½ teaspoons celery seed
1 tablespoon whole allspice

Simmer cucumbers in 4 cups of vinegar, plus all of salt and ½ cup sugar, for 15 minutes, or just until yellow (don't overcook). Discard liquid. Boil remaining vinegar, 3 ½ cups of remaining sugar and spices until boiling rapidly. Pour over cucumbers in sterilized jars and seal with sterilized lids. Let stand for a week or more before eating.

From John Littlefield who worked in our Washington office comes two recipes —

MUSTARD BOUQUET PICKLES

3 quarts sliced cucumbers (4 or 5 cucumbers, cut ½ to ¾ -inch thick)
1 medium cauliflower, broken into small pieces
1 quart pickling onions (to clean onions pour boiling water over and remove skins)

Keep each item in a separate pan. Pour hot brine of 2 ½ tablespoons salt to 1 quart water over each individual pan of vegetables. Leave 24 hours.

Make the following and have hot and ready:
Cook until thick:
½ cup dry mustard
4 cups vinegar
6 cups white sugar
¾ cup flour
1 tablespoon tumeric
1 tablespoon celery seed

Have the containers of cucumbers, cauliflower and onions, the mustard sauce, a seive or colander, and one *large* kettle ready. Drain the brine from the vegetables. (Individually heat and pour the brine over each individual pan of vegetables. Drain each very well.) Put the drained vegetables in the *hot* sauce in one large kettle, mix and pour into sterilized jars. Seal.

These pickles are very good but should be eaten within three or four months.

Dorothy Palmer and Theresa have the same birthday. Dorothy is always thoughtful to remember our daughter with something she has made, such as a handknit sweater or a needlepoint sampler. Thank you, Dorothy.

DOROTHY PALMER'S SWEET OR SOUR PICKLES

Pack sterilized quart jars with medium sized, scrubbed cucumbers.

Add:
1 tablespoon salt
1 tablespoon pickling spices
1 teaspoon prepared horseradish
Scant ¼ teaspoon powdered alum
1 cup vinegar

Fill jars with cold water. Seal with heated dome lids. Let stand six to eight weeks, or as long as you like. 24 to 48 hours before using, pour off brine and discard. Wash pickles and jar. Cut the cucumbers into slices or chunks and put back into the jar that has been well rinsed. Add 1 cup white granulated sugar, put lid back on and shake several times to dissolve sugar. Leave out where you will remember to shake jar occasionally. After the second day, or longer, they will be ready to eat.

This pickle recipe is so simple and really good that it, too, is reMARKable. If you don't care for them as spicy as these, you can remove the red peppers that come in the pickling spices. You can also add small pickling onions, cauliflower or garlic. It is possible to make one jar or several depending on the supply of cucumbers on hand. Dorothy says, "Don't be alarmed if they turn gray-green — they're okay."

From Leane Ellis in Birmingham, Alabama.

PICKLED OKRA

1 quart white vinegar
1 pint water
⅓ cup salt

Put in each jar before packing okra:
1 clove garlic for each jar
1 hot pepper for each jar
1 teaspoon mixed pickling spices

Bring vinegar, salt and water to boil. Let simmer 5 minutes. Pack jars firmly with small, young okra. Do not remove stems. Pour hot vinegar mixture over okra. Sprinkle spices on top. Seal. Chill before serving.

Maxine, who was for years the women's editor, still does the food section for **The Oregon Statesman** *in Salem. She says she's had this recipe in her files for years. Yes, it's the one I wanted, Maxine. Thanks.*

PLUM CHUTNEY — FROM MAXINE BUREN

Cook 4 quarts plums in mild vinegar to cover until tender, but not soft. Add ½ cup chopped onion, ½ cup brown sugar, ½ cup chopped raisins, 2 tablespoons mustard seed and 4 tablespoons scraped ginger root (or candied ginger); salt, pepper, paprika to taste; and grated rind of 2 lemons and the juice of 1 lemon. Cook slowly, until thick, and seal in jars.

QUICK DILL PICKLES

Pack cucumbers into sterilized jars. For each quart jar use 2 heads of dill, 1 grape leaf, 2 cloves garlic, 2 red peppers. Over this pour a solution of 1 quart vinegar, 2 quarts water, ⅔ cup salt, which has been boiled. Seal jars and put in water bath. Count time when water returns to boiling, continuing to boil gently for 15-20 minutes. Let jars cool in water. Remove jars and turn upside down until completely cool.

SPICED APRICOT PICKLES — FROM MOLLIE ALLEN STRAND

2 cups dried apricots
Water
2 cups sugar
6 tablespoons cider vinegar
2-4 whole cloves
1 ½ teaspoons mustard seed
2 sticks cinnamon

Wash apricots. Put in a saucepan and cover with water. Boil gently for 5 minutes. Add sugar, vinegar, cloves, mustard seed and cinnamon sticks. Simmer gently until apricots are tender but still hold shape — about 15 minutes longer. Cover and refrigerate in the syrup until ready to serve, or seal them while still hot in sterilized jars. Makes about three 8-ounce jars. Refrigerated, pickles will keep for about 2 weeks without sealing.

WANDA'S GARLIC DILL PICKLES (Hot)

Wash and soak cucumbers overnight in plain water. Drain. Pack in sterilized jars. Add to each jar one clove garlic, one or two red peppers, one head dill. Make the following solution and pour into jars. This is enough for six quarts:
2 quarts water
1 quart vinegar
¾ cup plain salt
1 teaspoon alum
2 tablespoons horseradish

Boil before pouring over cucumbers. Seal and let stand for six weeks.

Pies

The art of making presentable pie crusts is still to be perfected. You may notice I have gone to meringue and cracker crusts in this section.

Mark likes pie when it's freshly baked ... guess who eats the rest!

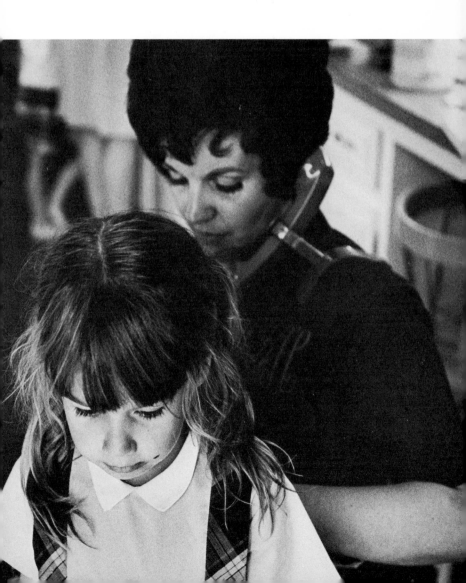

Since coming to Washington, I have had the privilege of meeting "Dear Abby," who is very warm and charming and gracious. So, this recipe, clipped from her column a long time ago, is more meaningful now. I am glad to need only her recipes for pies!

ABBY'S PECAN PIE

1 cup white corn syrup
1 cup dark brown sugar
⅓ teaspoon salt
⅓ cup melted butter
1 teaspoon vanilla
3 whole eggs
1 heaping cup shelled pecans

Mix syrup, sugar, salt, butter, vanilla. Mix in slightly beaten eggs. Pour into 9-inch unbaked pie shell. Sprinkle pecans over filling. Bake in 350° oven approximately 45 minutes.

This is one of those light-as-a-feather, melt-in-your-mouth, pies. It is Mark's Aunt Birdie's recipe, and you can count on any of her recipes. Remember those from the first book?

AUNT BIRDIE'S LEMON CHIFFON PIE

1 package piecrust mix
2 envelopes unflavored gelatin
2 cups sugar
¼ teaspoon salt
8 egg yolks
1 cup lemon juice
2 tablespoons grated lemon peel
8 egg whites
1 cup heavy cream, whipped
1 cup water

Prepare piecrust as package label directs; shape into ball and roll out to fit an 11-inch pie plate. Refrigerate 1 hour. Preheat oven to 450°. Prick entire surface of shell evenly. Bake shell 15 minutes, or until golden brown. Cool on wire rack.

In top of double boiler, combine gelatin with 1 cup sugar and the salt. In small bowl, beat egg yolks with lemon juice and 1 cup water just until combined. Stir into gelatin mixture. Cook over boiling water, stirring constantly, until gelatin is dissolved and mixture is thickened — 10-12 minutes. Remove from water; stir in lemon peel. Set in bowl with ice cubes and let cool, stirring occasionally, until mixture is thick and mounds when dropped from spoon (about 30 minutes). In large bowl, with electric mixer at high speed, beat egg whites until soft peaks form when beater is slowly raised. Gradually add remaining sugar, 2 tablespoons at a time, beating well after each addition. Continue beating until stiff peaks form. With electric mixer at low speed, or with a wire whisk, fold gelatin mixture and whipped cream into egg whites, just until combined. Turn half of mixture into baked pie shell, refrigerate, along with rest of mixture, 10 minutes. Then turn remaining mixture into pie shell, mounding in center. Refrigerate until firm, at least 3 hours. If desired, decorate top with whipped cream and lemon slices before serving.

Makes 12 servings.

I thought this was a new find; but in going through my files, I noted one or two like it. It's rich, so a little goes a long way.

CHOCOLATE CANDY PIE

20 regular-size marshmallows
½ cup milk
2 bars (3¾-ounce size) milk chocolate with almonds
1½ cup heavy cream
9-inch prepared graham cracker pie shell

In medium saucepan, combine marshmallows and milk. Cook over low heat, stirring occasionally, until marshmallows are melted. Add chocolate bars, broken in pieces, and continue cooking, stirring constantly, until chocolate is melted. Remove from heat. Pour into a 9 x 9 x 2-inch pan. Place in freezer, to cool quickly — about 10 minutes. Pour into pie shell. Refrigerate pie until well chilled (at least 3 hours).

IRIS' STRAWBERRY MILE HIGH PIE

Beat 2 egg whites with 1 cup sugar as you would a meringue. Add 1 tablespoon lemon juice. Add 2 small, or 1 large, package frozen strawberries, still frozen. Beat *15 minutes* by the clock, at high speed. Pour into a cracker crust, or baked pie shell. *Freeze* pie.

Iris says this may be served in sherbet or parfait glasses. Perhaps this is because it may not holds its shape!

My husband occasionally invites me out to dinner, and on more than one occasion I have had to use my "mad money" to help pay the bill. Somehow, even this great statesman has never lost that "absent-minded professor" characteristic. Issues are more important to him than money.

During the last week I was working on this book, Mark took me to dinner at Black-beards, a cozy restaurant here in Washington, and this Lime Pie of Anita Bryant's is similar to the one we ate there that evening. (Just to be on the safe side, I stopped at our local drugstore on my way to the Capitol to meet him and cashed a check, in case we had to go "Dutch Treat.")

KEY LIME PIE CRUST

1 cup graham cracker crumbs
2 or 3 tablespoons melted butter
2 tablespoons sugar

Mix in pie pan and press to pie pan until formed to pan. Put in the middle of the oven; heat in 350° oven for approximately 10 minutes; watch closely so as not to burn.

KEY LIME PIE FILLING

1 can sweetened condensed milk
3 egg yolks
½ cup lime juice

Mix together and pour into cooled graham cracker pie crust and set in refrigerator for at least one hour.

Topping:
½ pint heavy cream — whipped
2 teaspoons powdered sugar
1 teaspoon vanilla

Combine and spread over Key Lime Pie and refrigerate or freeze to eat.

LOIS OBERDORF'S FUDGE PIE

¼ pound butter, cream with
⅔ cup granulated sugar, add
1 ounce melted, unsweetened chocolate, and
1 teaspoon vanilla
2 eggs, added 1 at a time, and beat mixture 5 minutes
after each egg is added.

Pour into baked graham cracker crust. Refrigerate for
at least 4 hours — or overnight.

Important: Beating each egg for 5 minutes after it is
added to the other ingredients (at quite a high speed)
is the key to the success of this pie.

Serve with whipped cream.

*Lois says she makes this recipe three times to
fill two 9-inch pie shells. She got this recipe
from Marlene Starr whose husband, Chet,
works for Young Life (a Christian lay
group) in Seattle. Marlene and Chet are
long-time friends of ours.*

Here is another of Mary Jane Dellenback's good recipes. She made over one hundred tarts for our Inaugural Brunch. She's really a good neighbor!

LEMON CURD TARTS

2 cups granulated sugar
¼ pound butter
5 eggs
Juice of 3 lemons
Grated rind of 2 lemons
Tart shells (see below)

Beat eggs until very light. Combine all ingredients and cook over hot water for 20 minutes, until thick. Refrigerate.

Tart Shells:
½ pound butter
4 tablespoons granulated sugar
2 teaspoons vanilla
2 cups cake flour

Cream butter and sugar thoroughly. Combine all ingredients well and mix with fingers. Press into fluted tart pans. Bake at 350° for 15 minutes. Fill cooled tart shells with cooled lemon filling.

Make tart shell recipe twice for all of lemon filling.

Lois and Ben Weiler have been long-time political supporters, not only in getting out the vote, but with their prayers, as well.

LOIS WEILER'S FROZEN LEMON PIE

2 egg yolks (saving 1 white for later)
½ cup sugar (reserving 1 tablespoon for later)
¼ cup lemon juice (scant)
¼ lemon rind (cut in strips with white pulp removed)
1 package vanilla wafers, crushed fine
1 cup heavy cream, whipped

Cook first four ingredients in double boiler until thick, stirring constantly. Cool and remove rind. Whip egg white until stiff to hold peak. Add 1 tablespoon sugar (saved from above). Whip heavy cream and fold into lemon mixture, then fold in egg white. Spread ½ of crushed vanilla wafers in bottom of greased 10-inch pie plate. Add filling and sprinkle remainder of vanilla wafers on top. Freeze overnight.

JANE APPLING'S FROZEN LEMON PIE

3 eggs
½ cup plus 2 tablespoons sugar
Juice of 1 lemon (large)
1 cup whipping cream
Graham cracker crumbs

Separate eggs. Beat yolks, ½ cup sugar and lemon juice until thick and light in color. Beat cream and refrigerate. Beat egg whites until stiff and add the 2 tablespoons sugar. Mix all together lightly. Pour into ice tray which has been lined with graham cracker crumbs. Sprinkle on top also. Freeze on high for at least 3 hours.

Jane Appling served this at a dinner when she and Howell (Tiny) entertained for us before we were married. At that time Howell was a successful businessman who, after Mark appointed him to be Secretary of State, went on to become one of Oregon's most popular political figures. Even today, in his retirement from public office, Howell commands a large army of supporters, his attractive wife, Jane, always at his side.

B. J. Noles, one of our hometown society editors, gave me this recipe.

B. J. covered the dinner for their majesties, the King and Queen of Nepal, when they visited Oregon. I tried to make her guess what the menu would be, but being the good reporter she is, she found out anyway. I wasn't as good at finding out about her pie until she sent the recipe. It is a conversation piece!

MAKE 'EM GUESS PIE

3 egg whites, beaten stiff
1 cup sugar (added gradually to egg whites while they are being beaten)
1 teaspoon baking powder
1 teaspoon vanilla
20 crackers (saltines), rolled
½ cup walnuts or pecans

Butter a 9-inch pie pan. Beat egg whites, gradually adding sugar, until stiff peaks are formed. Add baking powder. Fold in vanilla, crackers and nuts. Bake 40 minutes at 325°. Serve with whipped cream.

Another do-ahead, calorie-filled pie . . .

MILE HIGH ICE CREAM PIE

1 baked 9-inch pastry shell, cooled
1 pint chocolate ice cream, softened
1 pint mocha ice cream, softened

Spread chocolate ice cream in pie shell; top with layer
of mocha ice cream; place in freezer.

Meringue:
4 egg whites
½ teaspoon vanilla
¼ teaspoon cream of tartar
½ cup sugar

Beat egg whites with vanilla and cream of tartar till
soft peaks form. Gradually add sugar, beating till
stiff and glossy. Spread meringue over ice cream,
carefully sealing to edge of pastry. Bake in very hot
oven — 475° for 2-3 minutes or till meringue is lightly browned. Freeze pie several hours, or overnight.
To serve, cut in wedges and drizzle with chocolate
sauce.

Chocolate Sauce:
In saucepan, heat 4 squares (4 ounces) unsweetened
chocolate and ¾ cup water together over low heat,
stirring constantly until chocolate is smooth and melted. Stir in 1 cup sugar and dash of salt. Simmer till
slightly thickened, about 5 minutes. Remove chocolate
mixture from heat, blend in 6 tablespoons butter or
margarine and 1 teaspoon vanilla. Serve warm over
wedges of pie.

Here is another contribution from a campaign chairman's wife. Mrs. Tripp's husband is the mayor of Albany, Oregon. This recipe is worth more than time or money.

MRS. RUSSELL TRIPP'S MT. JEFFERSON HUCKLEBERRY PIE

3 cups huckleberries (thaw and drain, if frozen)
1 cup granulated sugar
2 tablespoons flour
¼ teaspoon salt
1 teaspoon lemon juice (more to suit taste)
2 eggs, separated (use 3 if individual pies are made)
1 baked, 9-inch pie shell (or 4 individual crusts)
2 tablespoons powdered sugar

Mix together huckleberries, sugar, flour, salt, lemon juice and egg yolks. Cook over boiling water for 10 minutes, or until thickened, stirring constantly. Cool slightly. Turn into baked shell and cover with meringue made of whites of eggs and powdered sugar. Bake in moderate oven (350°) about 15 minutes until delicately browned.

P.S. Blackberries may also be used.

This is one of Mark's favorites . . .

ORANGE CHIFFON PIE

1 package, plus ½ tablespoon, unflavored gelatin
1 ¾ cups fresh orange juice
⅔ cup sugar
¼ teaspoon salt
¼ cup lemon juice
1 tablespoon grated orange peel
1 cup heavy cream
½ cup egg whites, stiffly beaten

In the top part of a double boiler, soften gelatin in ½ cup of orange juice. Add sugar and salt. Place over boiling water; stir until gelatin is dissolved. Remove from heat, add remaining orange juice, lemon juice and orange peel. Chill until mixture is partially thickened, then beat until light and fluffy.

Whip cream until stiff. Fold into gelatin mixture. Fold in stiffly beaten egg whites. Chill until slightly thickened, about 20 minutes. Pour into your favorite graham cracker crust. Chill until set. Top with whipped cream; garnish with thin orange slices.

I looked and looked for this recipe, and of course didn't find it in time, for my last book. So, here it is — Pumpkin pie is a campaign-time favorite, anyway.

PUMPKIN PIE TOPPING

Slice fresh dates and marinate them in a little orange juice. Add a touch of finely chopped candied ginger or grated orange rind. Fold into sweetened whipped cream.

For those of you who stock brandy, I'm told a small amount added to the orange juice gives it a different flavor.

Serve on your favorite pumpkin pie.

*And from Gerry Frank's cook, Sig, comes
this unusual pie crust. She serves it with this
Chocolate Chiffon Pie filling, but I think it
would be good with almost any other flavor . . .*

PEANUT PIE CRUST

1 cup flour
½ teaspoon baking powder
½ teaspoon salt
⅓ cup salted peanuts, crushed fine
3 tablespoons shortening
3-4 tablespoons water

Mix, using standard method, and roll out on a floured
pastry cloth to an 11-inch circle. Fit pastry loosely
into a 9-inch pie pan. Bake at 400° for 15 minutes,
or until brown. Cool.

CHOCOLATE CHIFFON PIE

1 tablespoon gelatin
1 cup milk
2 squares chocolate
¾ cup sugar
2 eggs, separated
¼ teaspoon cinnamon
½ teaspoon vanilla
¾ cup whipping cream

Soften gelatin in ¼ cup milk. Melt 2 squares chocolate in top of double boiler. Add sugar, egg yolks and
cinnamon. Blend in ¾ cup milk. Cook over boiling
water till mixture thickens and will coat a spoon,
stirring constantly. Add vanilla and chill until mixture
begins to thicken. Beat egg whites till stiff, gradually
adding 2 tablespoons sugar. Whip cream and fold into
stiff beaten egg whites. Then fold into chocolate mixture which has been beaten smooth. Pour into cooled
baked pie shell. Chill 2-3 hours before serving. Top
with whipped cream.

Eleanore Voss, whose husband is the president of a Portland bank, gave me this recipe. It is worth "a million" in any recipe account!

REFRIGERATOR PIE

½ pound vanilla wafers, rolled fine
3 tablespoons melted butter
½ cup softened butter
2 cups powdered sugar
3 eggs, well beaten
½ cup chopped nuts
1 cup crushed pineapple, drained
½ pint pastry cream, whipped

Mix the wafer crumbs with the melted butter and line a large glass pie pan with this mixture, saving some of crumbs for later to sprinkle on top. Cream the softened butter and sugar thoroughly and beat in the eggs. Spread this over the crust and sprinkle with the chopped nuts. Then spread the crushed pineapple (drained) over all. Spread with the whipped cream in rough swirls and sprinkle with the remaining crumbs. Let stand in the refrigerator for 12 hours. Other fruits may be substituted, depending on the season. Strawberries are especially good.

Rices & Other Starches

For a well-balanced plate, always include a "starch" dish. This is good nutritionally and helps fill up the more hungry eaters at your table.

This is a very unusual rice dish — can be prepared for baking ahead of time.

AUNT DOROTHY'S RICE CASSEROLE

4 cups cooked rice
1 pound Monterey Jack cheese, cubed or grated
1 bunch chopped green onions (using tops as well)
3 stalks celery, chopped
1 can green chiles, chopped

Mix ingredients in 2-quart buttered casserole dish with cover. Bake at 350° for 45 minutes to 1 hour, or until bubbly and all cheese is melted.

Makes 10-12 servings.

This is one of my favorite "starch dishes."

GRITS AND CHEESE CASSEROLE

2 eggs
4 cups water
½ teaspoon salt
1 cup grits
Cream (enough to make 1 cup with eggs)
3 tablespoons butter
1 clove garlic, mashed
1 ½ cups grated cheddar cheese

Put salt in water, bring to a boil. Add grits and cook about 20 minutes. Beat eggs and add enough cream to make 1 cup. To the cooked grits add butter, egg and cream mixture, garlic and 1 cup grated cheese. Pour into buttered 2-quart glass casserole. Sprinkle remaining ½ cup of cheese on top. Bake at 325° for about 45 minutes.

Makes 8-10 servings.

Mrs. Paul Poling sent me a noodle recipe—
Thanks, Thanks, Thanks! (I like the "½ egg
shell of water" in this recipe!)

MABEL POLING'S NOODLES

2 eggs
½ egg shell of water
1 teaspoon salt
Flour

Beat eggs and water. Add salt and all the flour you
can knead in. Roll into two wheels. Let these dry a
while, but roll up before dough cracks. Slice as thin
as possible. Boil in salt water. Store in a paper bag if
you wish to keep a while before cooking.

MARY McCLUER'S PAN DE ELOTE

1 can (1 pound) cream style corn
1 cup biscuit mix
1 egg, beaten
2 tablespoons melted butter
2 tablespoons sugar, optional
½ cup milk
1 can (14 ounces) green chiles, sliced
½ pound Monterey Jack cheese, thinly sliced

In bowl combine corn, biscuit mix, egg, butter, sugar,
milk; mix these ingredients well. Turn half of this
batter into a well-greased 8 x 8-inch glass baking
dish. Cover with chiles, then cheese slices, spreading
remaining batter over cheese.

Bake at 400° for 20 minutes, or until done and golden
brown.

NOODLES ROMANOFF

2 packages (8 ounce size) egg noodles
3 cups large curd cottage cheese
2 cloves garlic, chopped or mashed
2 teaspoons Worcestershire sauce
2 cups thick, cultured sour cream
1 bunch green onions, finely chopped
½ teaspoon Tabasco
1 cup grated Parmesan cheese

Cook noodles in boiling water until noodles are
tender. Drain. Combine cooked noodles, cottage
cheese, garlic, Worcestershire, sour cream, grated
onions and Tabasco. Put mixture into a buttered
casserole; sprinkle grated cheese over the top. Bake
in a 350° oven for 25 minutes.

Makes 18 servings.

*When General Harold K. Johnson was
head of the Joint Chiefs of Staff, he came
to Oregon to speak at the Governor's Prayer
Breakfast. Mrs. Johnson sent me this recipe
which is delicious. Do be sure to test the
center with a knife to be sure it is done.
My first try was a bit soupy in the center.*

ONION BREAD

1 package (8 ounces) corn muffin mix
1 can cream style corn
1 egg
1 large onion, finely chopped
3 tablespoons butter
¾ cup grated cheddar cheese
Sour cream

Combine first three ingredients and put into a 6-cup
greased casserole. Saute the large onion (chopped) in
3 tablespoons butter. Mix this with grated cheddar
cheese and pour over top of corn muffin mixture.
Spread sour cream evenly over top of this and bake at
400° for 30-45 minutes, or until knife inserted in
center comes out clean.

Makes 8 servings.

This is one of the best side dishes I have ever tasted. The Farm Women of Lebanon, Pennsylvania, cooked for a GOP fund-raising dinner during the 1968 campaign. Mrs. Dubble was kind enough to send me the recipe. Lebanon is in the heart of the Pennsylvania Dutch country.

POTATO FILLING

4 cups cooked potatoes
2 or 3 cups bread crumbs (cubes)
1 cup plus 1 tablespoon milk
1 cup celery, chopped
½ cup onion, chopped
¼ cup butter
3 or 4 eggs
1 tablespoon parsley, chopped fine
Salt and pepper to taste

Cook potatoes and mash. Saute celery and onion in ¼ cup butter until tender. When just about finished add 1 tablespoon chopped parsley, chopped. Add milk, eggs, salt, and pepper and bread cubes to potatoes, with sauteed celery and onions. Mix all ingredients together until of a consistency a little thinner than mashed potatoes. Put in a buttered casserole and dot with butter. Bake at 350° until golden brown. You may desire to add more butter. One-half cup would make a richer mixture.

Salads & Salad Dressings

Salads provide not only the variety, the extra bit of food on a buffet, but to me are probably the most creative and colorful part of lunch or dinner. Some salads can be a meal in themselves while others are the "supporting actors" . . . take your choice.

*This is one green salad that Mark really
likes — another of Anita Bryant's top recipes.*

ANITA BRYANT'S WILTED SPINACH SALAD

1 pound fresh spinach
3 green onions and tops, thinly sliced
5 slices bacon, diced and cooked, crisp
2 tablespoons vinegar
1 teaspoon sugar
Coarse ground pepper
1 tablespoon lemon juice
½ teaspoon salt
¼ cup grated Parmesan cheese
1 hard cooked egg, chopped

Wash spinach and tear off stems; pat dry and tear into
bite-size pieces in bowl. Add onions and sprinkle
liberally with pepper; cover with foil and chill thoroughly. At serving time, fry bacon, add vinegar,
lemon juice, sugar and salt; add spinach mixture and
toss just until leaves are coated and slightly wilted.
Sprinkle with Parmesan cheese and hard boiled egg.

This recipe was served in the Senate Dining Room one spring, courtesy of some members of the California delegation to Congress.

ARTICHOKES SEVILLA

Trim artichokes, cutting off stem, top and clipping each outer leaf. Steam in tightly-covered pan in 1-2 inches of water, to which has been added:
1 tablespoon vegetable oil
Salt to taste
1 bouillon cube
Good dash instant garlic powder
Tarragon
Summer Savory
Marjoram
Juice of 1 lemon
Squeezed lemon peels (depending upon size and freshness)
Cook about 35 minutes.

Marinade:
½ cup vegetable oil
½ cup lemon juice, more or less
3 or 4 tablespoons of capers with juice from bottle
1 tablespoon prepared mustard dressing
1 teaspoon French Dijon prepared mustard
Dash of Worcestershire sauce
Liberal portion parsley flakes and dehydrated red and green peppers

Drain the artichokes. While still hot, place on platter or dish with a lip. Pour marinade over artichokes, making sure lots of marinade gets between leaves. Insert capers between leaves. Chill before serving.

*This is another of Iris' creative cooking
tricks — wouldn't you agree?*

AVOCADO AND FROZEN MAYONNAISE

4 small tomatoes
1 ¼ teaspoons grated onion
1 cup mayonnaise
Salt
Paprika
Cayenne pepper
Pepper
4 avocados, cut in half, lengthwise

Peel tomatoes and chop fine, combine with grated
onion and fold in mayonnaise. Season to taste. Pour
this mixture into freezing tray and freeze quickly,
without stirring, about 1 ½ hours. Serve a cube in
hollow of half avocado.

*This is the way it was given to me. You'll
have to figure out your own amounts. Avocados do taste good with it.*

AVOCADO MARINADE — FAIRMONT HOTEL

Wine vinegar
Olive oil
Shallots
Garlic

Make a base of above ingredients. Finish with parsley
or chives and sharp pimientos.

This is the dressing that Mark liked so well at the University of Arizona Student Union. He's very good about collecting recipes for me.

BUTTERMILK SALAD DRESSING

½ cup buttermilk
4 teaspoons prepared horseradish
1 teaspoon sugar
⅛ teaspoon dry mustard
⅛ teaspoon salt
Few grains pepper

Combine all ingredients and chill thoroughly. Makes about ½ cup dressing.

Florist Helene Schucking makes salads that are almost as beautiful as flower arrangements. The combination of beets with the string beans is delicious . . .

CARDINAL BEET SALAD

1 package lemon flavored gelatin
1 cup boiling water
¾ cup beet juice
1 tablespoon vinegar
½ tablespoon salt
1 tablespoon onion juice, or 1 grated onion
1 tablespoon horseradish
1 cup diced or string beets
¾ cup diced celery

When gelatin is slightly cool, combine rest of ingredients in ring mold. Chill thoroughly. At serving time, unmold salad, serve with your choice of dressing and garnish with cut Blue Lake string beans.

Wanda Fisher and Iris Collins served this at a shower they had for me before Visko was born. It is a great party dish — tastes good and looks pretty, too.

CHICKEN DINNER SALAD

One day before, simmer:
4 boned, skinned, medium-size chicken breasts in 1 can (13¾ ounces) chicken broth, covered, for 30 minutes, or until fork tender. Refrigerate in broth. About 30 minutes before serving, remove chicken from broth.

Mix:
½ of a 3-ounce package cream cheese
2 tablespoons mayonnaise
1 teaspoon lemon juice
¼ teaspoon lemon peel
⅛ teaspoon salt
1 tablespoon snipped fresh dill

Use this mixture to spread over rounded side of each chicken breast. On each of four supper plates, arrange 2 or 3 romaine leaves. Top with a thick tomato slice, sprinkled with seasoned salt; then top with a chicken breast and sprinkle a few toasted slivered almonds and a bit of snipped fresh dill. Garnish with a peeled avocado, pitted and cut into eighths. Pass your favorite French or Italian dressing.

This is a good summer supper salad. Serve with peach halves.

CURRY-CHICKEN RICE SALAD

1 cup uncooked rice
2 cups chicken broth
2 cups diced, cooked chicken
2 cups finely chopped celery
1 tablespoon finely minced onion
1 cup mayonnaise
¼ cup lemon juice
1 teaspoon salt
¼ teaspoon pepper
Paprika
1 teaspoon curry powder

Cook rice according to package directions, using chicken broth in place of water and omitting salt. Cool. Add chicken, celery, and onion. Add mayonnaise, lemon juice, salt, pepper and curry to rice mixture and toss well. Chill. Sprinkle with paprika. Makes 6-8 servings.

Garnish with peach halves.

Before our Oregon Trade Mission left for Japan, Mr. and Mrs. Ted Bruno entertained for the group. Dean Bruno filled the center of this Mustard Ring with a finely chopped cole slaw.

DEAN'S MUSTARD RING

4 eggs, separated
½ cup sugar
1 ½ tablespoons dry mustard
1 ½ envelopes unflavored gelatin
¾ cup vinegar
¼ cup water
1 cup whipping cream

Soak gelatin in ¼ cup cold water. Combine egg yolks, sugar, gelatin, mustard and vinegar in double boiler. Cook until mixture forms a custard. Cool mixture. Beat whites until stiff. Whip cream until stiff. Fold both into cooled custard mixture. Pour into mold and chill until firm.

(If large mold is used, increase recipe.)

DILLED BLUE LAKE BEANS

3 No. 2 ½ cans Blue Lake beans
½ cup white vinegar
½ cup sugar
½ cup water
1 teaspoon dillweed

Combine all ingredients but the beans. Drain beans and add to marinade. Marinate at least overnight — 3 days is all right, too — and serve chilled.

*At the Fat Farm, while we were slimming
on 100 calories a day, Dorotha gave us this
recipe. Imagine how good it sounded then,
and it tasted even better later. Try it and
see.*

DOROTHA'S NON-DIET LAYERED SALAD

Layer the following ingredients:
1 thin layer shredded lettuce
1 thin layer thinly sliced celery
1 thin layer blanched peas (cooked and cooled)
1 thin layer shredded carrots
1 thin layer thinly sliced onion rings

Sprinkle lightly with granulated sugar (1 teaspoon)
and dot with mayonnaise.
Repeat layers three times.
Sprinkle top with crumbled crisp bacon and paprika.

*This is an exceptionally zippy French dress-
ing from Grandmother Dovie.*

FRENCH DRESSING

1 cup ketchup
1 cup cider vinegar
1 cup vegetable oil
1 cup white sugar
1 teaspoon celery seed
2 cloves garlic, mashed
1 teaspoon Worcestershire sauce
1 teaspoon dry mustard

Mix all in blender. Always shake well before using.

My old college roommate, Charlotte Alexander Wendel, is so good about sending me recipes. Perhaps it's because we cooked so many cans of soup on a hot plate in our dormitory room to keep from starving!

FRENCH DRESSING

⅓ cup honey
½ cup vegetable oil
⅓ cup catsup
1 teaspoon salt
1 teaspoon paprika
1 onion, chopped fine
4 cloves garlic
¼ cup vinegar
1 tablespoon lemon juice

Combine all ingredients, placing toothpick through garlic so it can be removed after 24 hours. Shake well before serving.

POPPY SEED DRESSING

½ cup sugar
1 teaspoon salt
1 teaspoon dry mustard
1 teaspoon celery salt
1 teaspoon paprika
1 teaspoon onion juice
1 cup oil
¼ cup vinegar
Poppy seeds

Combine all ingredients in order given. Stir thoroughly. Put in covered jar and refrigerate until using.

From the kitchen of Mrs. Thomas J. O'Dwyer in Coos County, Oregon, comes . . .

FRESH MUSHROOM MARINADE IN TOMATO ASPIC RING

2 pounds fresh mushrooms
4 bunches green onions
4 lemons
Salt
Whole ground pepper
¼ cup oil (Olive oil)

Clean and slice fresh mushrooms into saucepan.
Chop green onions and add to the mushrooms. Squeeze
the juice of the lemons into mixture. Add Olive oil
and bring to a boil. Lower heat and allow to simmer
until mushrooms and onions have wilted to proper
doneness. Salt and pepper to taste and set aside to
cool. Chill in refrigerator. This may be prepared a few
days in advance of serving. Be sure to remove from refrigerator in time to allow oil to mix freely. The
mushroom marinade filler in a tomato aspic ring
makes an attractive buffet dish and is an exquisite
delight to the palate.

For those of you who don't remember how Grandmother used to make mayonnaise, Chef George Inglis submits this recipe . . .

HOME MADE MAYONNAISE

6 egg yolks
1 ½ teaspoons salt
Small pinch cayenne pepper
¼ pint water
1 quart vegetable oil
Juice of 1 lemon
3 tablespoons boiling water

Whip egg yolks with beater and gradually pour vinegar on the yolks. Add oil to the above in a trickle, while yolks are beating. Add juice of lemon and boiling water. *NOTE:* Use oil at room temperature. Do not add oil too fast to yolks. Hot water helps set the mayonnaise. Mayonnaise sets up firmer after 2 hours. If mayonnaise starts to break, take one yolk and few drops of vinegar and mix into the separated mayonnaise.

Little did I know when I tasted this delicious salad at one of Marian's "tasting" parties, that it would be good enough to win a trip to Europe for her.

MARIAN BURROS' POTATO SALAD

4 cups diced cooked potatoes
1 cup diced celery
½ cup diced onion
½ cup sweet pickle relish
4 hard cooked eggs, chopped
1 cup mayonnaise
½ teaspoon salt
Pepper to taste
1 envelope unflavored gelatin
1 tablespoon cold water
¾ cup pickle juice

Combine potatoes with celery, onions, pickles, eggs, mayonnaise, salt and pepper. Soften gelatin in cold water. Heat pickle juice and dissolve gelatin in it. Stir. Pour a thin layer of mixture into a 1 ½-quart mold. Chill until almost firm. Arrange carrot slices, pimiento-stuffed olives (sliced) and black olives (sliced) on chilled gelatin. Add remaining gelatin mixture to potato salad. Stir well to blend. Spoon over gelatin in mold. Chill until firm. Unmold to serve.

The year Betty Talmadge (Mrs. Herman Talmadge, of Georgia) and I were menu co-chairmen for the luncheon honoring Mrs. Lyndon B. Johnson, given by the Ladies of the Senate, we had a Hawaiian theme. This is the dressing we used on the chicken-lobster salad . . .

PAPAYA SEED DRESSING

1 cup sugar
1 tablespoon salt
1 teaspoon dry mustard
1 cup white wine or tarragon vinegar
1 cup salad oil
1 small onion, chopped
3 tablespoons fresh papaya seeds

Place dry ingredients and vinegar in blender. Turn on and gradually add salad oil and onion. When thoroughly blended, add papaya seeds. Blend only until seeds are size of coarse ground pepper. The piquant flavor of this dressing is excellent for fruit or tossed green salads.

Makes 3 cups of dressing.

Here is another of Marian Lowry Fischer's recipes . . .

PIMIENTO-BUTTERMILK DRESSING

1 clove garlic
1 package (3 ounces) pimiento cream cheese
1 cup buttermilk
¼ cup catsup
2 teaspoons Worcestershire sauce

Rub small mixing bowl with garlic. Mash in cream cheese. Gradually blend in buttermilk until smooth. Add remaining ingredients and mix well. Chill. Delicious with seafood or tossed green salads.

Makes 1 ½ cups dressing.

Mark is sure to like any salad if it has onions or whipped cream in it — not necessarily in the same salad . . .

ORANGE AND ONION SALAD

Basically, the skill and finesse required to produce an excellent salad depends upon the ability to select large, tasty oranges, and mild, preferably white, Bermuda onions.

Peel the rind from the oranges and be sure the under part of the rind is well removed. Slice the oranges in thin slices, not more than ¼-inch thick. Prepare the Bermuda onions for slicing and cut across the grain into thin slices of approximately the same maximum thickness as the orange slices, preferably a little thinner. Then prepare a bed of crisp lettuce and place alternate slices of orange and onion upon the leaves. Cover this with French dressing and chill and serve.

If the onions are a little strong, it is advisable to put them in a flat glass pan and sprinkle lemon juice generously over them as this will make them a little more palatable.

Combine this dressing with an equal part of mayonnaise and have a second dressing.

RUSSIAN DRESSING

Grate:
1 medium onion
2 cloves garlic

Add:
1 teaspoon salt
1 tablespoon Worcestershire sauce
½ cup sugar
⅓ cup catsup
1 cup vegetable oil

Mix and keep in refrigerator.

I don't know why this is called "secret" Thousand Island dressing, if Iris gave it to me! She should have known I'd pass on a recipe, if it was good!

SECRET THOUSAND ISLAND DRESSING

3 pints mayonnaise
1 cup catsup
1 tablespoon garlic powder (not salt)
2 ½ cups light cream
¼ cup sugar

Mix all ingredients in electric mixer and beat until well blended and fluffy. Yields approximately ½ gallon.

On a diet? Try this dressing for a change . . .

SLIM COTTAGE CHEESE DRESSING

1 cup trim cottage cheese
1 tablespoon chopped chives
½ teaspoon garlic salt
½ teaspoon salt
1 tablespoon lemon juice
½ cup buttermilk

Add, to taste:
Monosodium glutamate
Pepper
Caraway seed
Dry mustard
Curry
Paprika
Herbs

Blend together in blender and toss with salad greens.

Marian Burros brought this over for the same party for which she made the Sweet Pepper Rice Salad. She knows how every little bit helps when you're entertaining for more than 30 people.

SPICY PEACH CRANBERRY RING

1 No. 2 ½ can cling peach halves
1 teaspoon whole cloves
1 cinnamon stick, 3 inches
¼ cup vinegar
2 packages (3 ounce) lemon gelatin
1 cup fresh or frozen cranberries
½ unpeeled orange
⅓ cup sugar
1 ¾ cups hot water
1 package (3 ounces) cherry gelatin

Drain the peaches, reserving the syrup. Add enough water to syrup to make 1 ¾ cups. Add the cloves, cinnamon and vinegar to liquid and simmer, uncovered, 10 minutes. Add peaches; heat slowly for 5 minutes. Remove peaches. Place in 3-quart ring mold, cut side up. Strain syrup. Measure and add enough hot water to make 1 ⅔ cups. Add liquid to the lemon gelatin. Dissolve and pour over peaches. Refrigerate until almost firm. Meanwhile, put the cranberries and orange through a food chopper, using medium blade. Stir in the sugar. Add 1 ¾ cups hot water to cherry gelatin. Cool. Add cranberry mixture. Pour over almost jelled peach mixture. Chill until firm. Unmold to serve.

Makes 8 servings.

SWEET PEPPER RICE SALAD

4 cups cooked, cooled rice
3 large green peppers
1 large ripe tomato, cooked
2 ribs celery, diced
1 bunch scallions, sliced
2 cans anchovy fillets
2 tablespoons chopped parsley
¼ cup olive oil
2 tablespoons lemon juice
1 ½ teaspoon salt
¼ teaspoon pepper
2 cloves garlic, minced

Combine rice, diced peppers, tomato, celery, scallions, diced anchovies and parsley. Mix together oil and lemon juice, salt, black pepper and garlic and pour over mixture. Toss to mix. Refrigerate overnight to blend flavors. Toss again before serving.

From Jeanette Sulmonetti comes this recipe. She told me about it at a Chinese New Year's celebration. We have shared many community activities with the Judge and Mrs. Sulmonetti.

TUNA-NOODLE SALAD

Let set until syrupy:
2 packages lemon flavored gelatin
2 cups boiling water
Beat this mixture until light lemon color.

Then beat in:
2 cups mayonnaise
2 cans drained tuna fish
2 cans chicken noodle soup (cut up noodles in can)
1 small jar chopped stuffed olives
1 ½ cups chopped celery
Chill in 9 x 12-inch pan until firm.

Makes 12 servings.

Seafood

Now that our "legal voting residence" is located in Newport, Oregon — on the beautiful Oregon coast — I expect that we will be eating more seafood than ever. It certainly never tastes better than when it is freshly caught.

This recipe came from Mrs. D. E. Clark and is a zesty sauce for crab. Serve with green salad, french bread and lemon sherbet, as we often do when we're home in Newport.

BARBECUED CRAB

2 large crabs
4 tablespoons butter
1 large onion, chopped
3 cloves garlic, chopped
4 stalks celery, chopped
2 cups consomme
1 cup tomato juice
2 tablespoons Worcestershire
1 bay leaf
1 sprig parsley
4 peppercorns
4 tablespoons soy sauce
½ teaspoon Tabasco

Saute vegetables in butter, add other seasonings, consomme and tomato juice, except soy sauce. Cover and simmer 30 minutes. Strain and add soy sauce. Pour sauce over cracked crab in roasting pan, heat 20-30 minutes, basting occasionally.

Serves 4 (sometimes).

Who knows more about fish cooking than Dr. Ed Harvey of Astoria? No one!

BROILED SUPREME

1 to 1 ½ pounds halibut or other white flesh fish

Marinade:
1 tablespoon grated onion
2 tablespoons lemon juice
3 tablespoons melted butter

Arrange fish in shallow baking dish. Pour marinade over fish and let stand for about an hour. Broil until tender (12-15 minutes). Do not turn. Garnish with paprika and parsley.

This recipe was created for the Inaugural Brunch we gave in January, 1969. It will serve a crowd and can be extended by adding more milk.

CHINOOK SALMON CHOWDER

¼ pound butter
1 large onion, chopped
1 ½ cups diced celery
½ cup flour
½ gallon milk
8 cans (7 ¾ ounce) Chinook Salmon
4 cups cooked potatoes, diced
2 large plastic bags of mixed, frozen vegetables
1 teaspoon dillweed
1 tablespoon salt

Saute onion and celery in the butter until onion is tender. Stir in flour off the heat. Slowly add the milk, stirring. Remove the skin and any bones from the salmon and add, along with potatoes, mixed vegetables, dill and salt. At this point the chowder may be frozen. When ready to serve, cook until vegetables are done. Serve steaming hot, with crackers.

Makes 40 cups.

Another of Bob Ogles' tasty recipes . . .

CRAB LEGS ALMONDINE

Whip 1 cup of water with 3 eggs and salt and pepper to taste. Dip 12 crab legs (boiled and removed from shells) into mixture, then roll in flour. Again dip into egg mixture and roll in 1 cup bread crumbs. Fry in deep fat until golden brown. Serve topped with lemon butter and sliced almonds.

Makes 4 servings.

A family favorite . . .

DEVILED CRAB CASSEROLE

2 tablespoons butter or margarine
1 ½ cups chopped onion
1 ½ cups chopped celery
3 cups Dungeness crab meat, flaked
1 tablespoon Worcestershire sauce
Dash cayenne
½ teaspoon salt
¼ teaspoon pepper
½ teaspoon dry mustard
1 cup mayonnaise
1 cup cornflakes*

Melt butter in medium skillet. Add onion and celery;
saute until tender. Combine crabmeat, Worcestershire,
cayenne, salt, pepper, mustard and mayonnaise with
sauteed vegetables. Turn mixture into an 8 x 8 x 2-
inch baking dish. Sprinkle with cornflakes. Bake at
350° for 20 minutes.
Makes 6-8 servings.

*Croutons or buttered bread crumbs may be substi-
tuted. If you use bread crumbs, ¾ cups crumbs to 2
tablespoons butter will be sufficient.

*Dr. Joseph Trainer, of the University of
Oregon Medical School, gave me this recipe.
His low-fat diets, which include a number
of fish dishes, are sure to help you lose
weight. Here is one he told me about the
last time he put me on the scales.*

DOC'S DIET FISH DISH

Wrap 2 scallops in a fillet of sole (tie up). Steam 10
minutes. Spoon 2 tablespoons warmed frozen shrimp
soup, undiluted, over the fillets.

This fine fish dish was served at the luncheon Mrs. Richard Nixon gave for the Ladies of the Senate in 1969.

MR. HENRY HALLER'S RECIPE FOR CRABMEAT CAKES

2 tablespoons butter
1 tablespoon finely chopped shallots
1 tablespoon finely chopped green peppers

Saute shallots and green peppers in butter over low heat until soft. Add:
½ teaspoon dry mustard
1 pinch white pepper
1 dash Tabasco
1 dash Worcestershire sauce

Stir until mustard is well mixed and without lumps. Add:
2 tablespoons flour — stirring until smooth, then add slowly, constantly:
1 cup warm milk

Remove mixture from heat and cool slightly. Gently fold in:
1 cup fresh lump crab meat (canned or pasturized crab meat does not work as well with this recipe)
1 teaspoon finely chopped parsley
1 teaspoon finely chopped chives
1 tablespoon sherry
1 whole well-beaten egg

Pour mixture into another pan or bowl, cover and chill in refrigerator overnight. Using a spoon or ice cream scoop, dip out desired portion to form a ball. As each ball is shaped, roll it in:
1 cup crisp ground breadcrumbs (spread out on cutting board)

Flatten balls with a spatula to make the crab cake. Place on sheet pan and chill until ready to use. Just before serving, heat:
3 tablespoons butter
2 tablespoons corn oil
(Use heavy-duty saute pan, or iron skillet.)

Brown quickly (the crab cakes) on both sides and transfer to sheet pan. Place in preheated oven (375°) and bake for 10 minutes. Serve immediately.

Charlotte Wendell says, "This sounds like a ladies's dish, but men like it, too!"

HOT CRAB SOUFFLE

8-10 slices white bread
2 cups crab (preferably fresh)
1 cup mayonnaise
1 small onion, chopped
1 cup chopped celery
1 medium-sized green pepper, chopped
1 tablespoon minced parsley
1 teaspoon grated lemon peel
1 teaspoon salt
¼ teaspoon pepper
4 eggs
3 cups milk
1 can (10 ½ ounces) mushroom soup, undiluted
Grated Parmesan cheese

Dice 4 slices of bread and place in a buttered 3-quart shallow casserole, rectangular in shape. Mix together crab, mayonnaise, onion, celery, green pepper, parsley, lemon peel, salt and pepper. Arrange over bread mixture. Trim crusts from remaining slices and arrange over crab mixture. Beat eggs slightly, add milk to eggs, pour over bread. Cover with foil and place in refrigerator overnight.

Bake in slow oven — 325° — for 1 hour and 15 minutes. Heat undiluted cream of mushroom soup and spoon over baked souffle. Sprinkle generously with Parmesan cheese and then place under broiler for 2 minutes.

Makes 12 servings.

*Kathryn Laughton, who for years was "Mary Cullen" of the **Oregon Journal,** sent me this recipe . . .*

KATIE'S CRAB

Stuff mushroom caps with crab mixed with deviled sauce. Put in 400° oven for 20-25 minutes.

Deviled Sauce:
Chopped onion, mayonnaise, dry mustard, and dash of lemon juice and Worcestershire, to taste.

Dolly Merrill shared this recipe with the painting class. It's a good emergency or plan-ahead dish.

DOLLY MERRILL'S SHRIMP DELIGHT

1 can frozen soup, thaw 1 hour before preparing
1 can shrimp
1 cup sour cream
¼ cup minced onions, slightly sauteed
1 teaspoon curry, or more to taste

Mix all ingredients and warm. Put over cooked rice, sprinkle with coconut. Garnish with parsley, hard boiled eggs, etc. Serve with spiced apricot.

Makes 5-6 servings.

This "Sauce Tartare" is delicious with other kinds of fish, too.

SALMON TARTARE

6 pounds salmon with head and tail

Wrap fish in cheesecloth. Lay on rack in fish kettle and add Court bouillon to cover. Bring to boil and simmer gently, 10-12 minutes to pound. Remove carefully and unwrap cheesecloth, laying fish on platter covered with paper towels to absorb liquid. Chill.

Court bouillon:
2 quarts water
1 onion, chopped
1 carrot, chopped
3 stalks celery, chopped
1 bay leaf
2 sprigs parsley
6 peppercorns
1 tablespoon salt
2 cloves (whole)

Bring ingredients to a boil in large kettle. Add 2 tablespoons white vinegar. Simmer covered for 30 minutes. This Court bouillon is suitable for poaching most fish.

Sauce Tartare:
½ large Bermuda onion
2 hard cooked egg yolks
1 green pepper
2 garlic dill pickles
Put these ingredients through a food chopper, then add:
2 cups mayonnaise
¼ cup chili sauce
¼ bottle prepared horseradish
1 tablespoon capers
½ clove garlic, minced
Salt and pepper
Dash cayenne
½ cup sour cream

Refrigerate. A few hours before serving, arrange fish on platter. Mask carefully with sauce. Sprinkle on riced hard-boiled egg whites. Garnish with Dungeness crab. Refrigerate until serving time.

*I liked this recipe because it's tasty, it uses a good Oregon product, **and** it's baked in custard cups.*

SALMON TIMBALLS

1 can (1 pound) red salmon
2 eggs
1 cup soft bread crumbs
2 tablespoons melted butter
¼ teaspoon salt
⅛ teaspoon pepper
1 teaspoon lemon juice
⅓ cup milk

Mince salmon, add well-beaten egg yolks, bread crumbs, melted butter, seasoning, lemon juice, milk. Fold in stiffly beaten egg whites and pour into buttered custard cups (or muffin pans). Bake over hot water until salmon is firm and top is golden brown crust. Bake at 350°. Turn out carefully and serve with olive sauce.

Olive Sauce:
4 tablespoons butter
4 tablespoons flour
2 cups milk
Salt and pepper
⅔ cup chopped ripe olives

Blend flour, butter, salt and pepper. Add milk. When thickened, add olives.

Makes 6 servings of salmon and sauce.

Senator Allen J. Ellender is one of the last of a breed of Southern Gentlemen in that exclusive club called the "U. S. Senate." Besides being an able legislator, he is a good cook. Here is one of his more famous recipes.

SENATOR ELLENDER'S SHRIMP AND CRAB GUMBO

2 pounds peeled and deveined shrimp (about 4 pounds shrimp in shell)
½ pound crab meat
3 slices bacon
½ cup diced, smoked ham
2 tablespoons flour
1 pound onions, finely chopped (about 2 cups)
1 cup finely chopped celery
½ cup finely chopped bell pepper
½ teaspoon grated lemon rind
¼ cup chopped parsley
½ lemon
1 pod garlic, finely chopped
Few dashes each, Tabasco and Worcestershire
Pinch thyme
1 bay leaf
Salt and pepper to taste
3 cups water
1 pound fresh okra, or 10-ounce package frozen okra
2 tablespoons bacon fat
¼ cup sliced green onion tops
Cooked rice

If shrimp is frozen, let thaw on paper toweling, so that excess moisture is absorbed. See that no shells or cartilage are left in crab meat. Cook bacon in a large saucepan or kettle; drain on paper towel. Add ham to bacon fet in pan and cook until browned; remove ham. Add flour to fat and cook over low heat, stirring constantly, to make a scorchy-tasting browned "roux." Gradually add onions and cook slowly until well browned and onions are reduced to pulp. Add celery and bell pepper and grated lemon rind. Trim white membrane from ½ lemon then chop and add to onion mixture. Add garlic, Worcestershire sauce, Tabasco, thyme, bay leaf, salt, pepper and water. Crumble bacon and add. Add ham. Cook slowly about 45 minutes. Meanwhile, if using fresh okra, clean and trim it. Slice okra and cook in bacon fat, stirring to prevent scorching or browning, until okra is no longer ropey. After sauce mixture has cooked about 45 minutes, add okra to vegetable mixture and continue to cook for about 20 minutes. Add shrimp and crab meat. Bring mixture to a boil and cook about 5 minutes or just long enough to cook shrimp. Add chopped parsley and green onion tops. Serve with cooked rice in soup plates.

Makes 8 main dish servings.

Mrs. John Sherman Cooper is responsible for this "Senate Creamed Crab" which was served at a lunchen honoring Mrs. Lyndon Johnson.

SENATE CREAMED CRAB

2 ½ pints heavy cream
10 tablespoons butter
4 tablespoons flour
4 tablespoons cooking sherry
3 egg yolks
4 pounds crab meat (Dungeness, of course)
Salt and pepper to taste

Set aside 2 tablespoons cream. Whip the cream remaining in a 2-quart saucepan. Bring it to a boil. Melt butter over low heat and add flour to make a thick paste. Add paste to cream. Mix well with wooden spoon and season with salt and pepper to taste. Set aside ½ pint of this sauce. Warm the crab meat in the oven for 4 minutes in 2 ounces of cooking sherry. In a glass pie baking dish (one which can be placed on the dinner table, also), pour ½ cup of sauce in bottom of the dish. Place a layer of whole pieces of crab meat, cover with a layer of sauce, add another layer of crab meat, and repeat sauce, repeat procedure again, making three layers of crab meat and sauce. Mix the 3 egg yolks, the 2 tablespoons of cream (reserved from above) and the ½ pint of sauce (reserved from above) to a paste consistency. Spread this mixture on top of the creamed crab meat. Put under the broiler until browned.

Makes 10-12 servings.

*Kim Witwer said, "Are you going to add that Shrimp Curry recipe?" I answered, "I almost forgot." She said, "I wouldn't forget **that** one!"*

SHRIMP CURRY — MY OWN

In a 2-quart copper baking dish, melt 1 cube of butter. Saute 1 small onion, finely chopped. Add 2 pounds of fresh, cleaned, cooked shrimp. Sprinkle over this about 2 teaspoons powdered curry. Stir and simmer for about 15-20 minutes. Serve with fluffy white rice and buttered peas. It's as simple as that.

*Jan Harden used to be the "Nancy Morris" of the **Oregonian** Hostess House. This is one of her favorite recipes for —*

TOMATO-CRAB BISQUE

1 can Bisque of Tomato soup
1 can Green Pea (without ham) soup
1 can Consomme
½ cup light cream
½ pound frozen crab (fresh when available)
½ cup cooking sherry

Thoroughly mix the undiluted soups with a whisk. Add the cream and crab and heat almost to boiling. Add the sherry right before serving. Makes 3 generous main dish servings or 6 appetizer-size servings.

Jan serves this with French bread and a tossed green salad with artichokes and vinegar and oil dressing for a very filling meal.

Vegetables

The response I received from owners of **ReMARKable Recipes** to send me good vegetable recipes was really gratifying. I have tried to pick out a good cross-sampling of recipes to include here.

Some recipes were not included because I misplaced the name of the sender — Have you ever tried to remember "who gave me this recipe"?

I promise to do a better job of filing for —

Even More ReMARKable Recipes!

One day as Peggy Goldwater and I were sew-
ing on layettes at Ladies of the Senate Red
Cross, I asked if I might use this recipe of
hers which I had clipped out during the 1964
campaign, when her husband was the Repub-
lican nominee for President. With a smile,
she said, "Sure." Many thanks, Peggy.

ARIZONA BEAN POT

1 pound pinto beans
Water
2 teaspoons salt
2 large onions, diced
4 cloves garlic, diced
1 can (7 ounces) green chiles, chopped
1 can (1 pound 14 ounces) tomatoes
1 can (6 ounces) taco sauce
½ teaspoon cumin seed

Soak beans overnight in cold water to cover. Drain
and wash beans, then cover with about 2 inches fresh
water. Add salt and cook over moderate heat for 1
hour, adding water, if needed. Combine onion, garlic,
chiles, tomatoes and taco sauce and stir into beans.
Stir in cumin and simmer 1 ½ hours.

Makes 6 servings.

If spicier beans are wanted, this is easily achieved by
adding a teaspoon or two of red chili powder.

Jean Grotewole, with whom I became acquainted while doing my graduate work at Stanford, sent me these delicious vegetable recipes in her Christmas card this year. Jean and her husband, Phil, were my refuge during the years I did residence work when I was on the job 24 hours a day and seven days a week. It was nice to have a hideaway on those every-other Sundays off.

ARTICHOKES

4 eggs
Salt and pepper
Dash Tabasco
6 soda crackers, crumbled
½ pound sharp cheddar cheese, grated
2 jars marinated artichoke hearts, finely chopped
1 clove garlic, crushed
Small amount chopped parsley (½ to 1 teaspoon)
½ medium-sized onion, chopped fine
Fry onion and garlic in a little oil from artichoke hearts. Beat eggs, add each ingredient, beating with a fork. Pour into lightly greased, 8 x 8-inch baking dish and bake at 325° for 35-45 minutes. Cool before slicing into squares. Either heat and serve, or freeze and then heat and serve.

Conrad Joyner is one of those bright scholars who combines the practical and the philosophical in his two jobs — professor at the University of Arizona, and on the City Council in Tucson. Ann Joyner is a good complement. She is aware and concerned, not only for people, but for family and friends. We were privileged to have them on the staff when Mark was governor of Oregon. On a recent trip to Tucson, Ann served us this dish with a Southwestern flavor.

ANN JOYNER'S CORN PUDDING

1 can cream-style corn
3 eggs, slightly beaten
½ small can Green Chiles
¾ cup yellow corn meal
¾ cup milk
¾ cup grated cheddar cheese
2 tablespoons sugar
2 tablespoons salad oil
Salt and pepper

Combine all of the above ingredients and pour into a greased 2-quart casserole. Bake about 1 hour at 350°, put foil over if it gets dry. This dish can be baked in the morning until almost set, and finished before dinner.

This is a good way to serve two vegetables at one time. Shredding the carrots does take time, but the end result is worth it.

AUNT DOROTHY'S BAKED CARROT AND CHEESE RING

3 cups finely shredded fresh carrots
⅓ cup finely diced celery
1 cup finely chopped onion
½ cup fine dry bread crumbs
1 cup shredded cheese
1 ½ cups medium white sauce
¾ teaspoon salt
⅛ teaspoon pepper
3 eggs, separated
1 cup cooked peas

Combine carrots, celery, chopped onion, bread crumbs, shredded cheese, white sauce (your favorite kind), salt and pepper. Beat egg yolks and add to carrot mixture. Mix well. Beat whites until stand in soft, stiff peaks. Fold egg whites into carrot mixture. Pour into well-greased 1 ½-quart ring mold. Place in a pan of hot water. Bake at 325° for 1 hour and 15 minutes. Remove from oven and let stand 10 minutes. Turn onto serving plate. Fill center with buttered, cooked peas and onions.

Makes 8 servings.

Another of Aunt Dorothy's carrot recipes. Even people who don't like cooked carrots will like the combination in this recipe. I think it's a nice idea to combine the fruit and marmalade with carrots.

AUNT DOROTHY'S PARTY CARROTS

2 cans baby carrots
2 small cans mandarin oranges, drained
1 jar orange marmalade
1 tablespoon butter

Butter 1 ½-quart covered casserole. Mix carrots and oranges and marmalade. Pour into buttered casserole, cover and heat through at 325° for 20 minutes.

My mother makes broccoli very palatable with this recipe.

BABA'S BROCCOLI DIP

Cook and drain 2 oboxes of chopped broccoli (frozen) in top of double boiler. Slowly stir in and melt 1 roll processed garlic cheese spread and 1 cup undiluted cream of mushroom soup. Stir until smooth. In skillet slowly melt 1 cube butter and saute a bunch of chopped green onions, ½ cup finely chopped green pepper, 2 large stalks celery, finely chopped, and 3 tablespoons chopped parsley. After this mixture is sauteed, add dash of garlic powder, Worcestershire sauce, and 2 tablespoons flour. Mix all of the above into the broccoli, then add a can of chopped mushrooms. Keep warm with a candle or sterno heat.

For a casserole, drain broccoli extra well and put Parmesan cheese and buttered crumbs on top.

Another way to serve two vegetables at once — attractively.

BABA'S HOT SPINACH ON TOMATO RINGS

2 packages (10-ounce) frozen chopped spinach
Butter or margarine (enough to grease baking dishes)
6 eggs, slightly beaten
1 ⅓ cups milk
1 medium onion, grated
Salt and pepper to taste
1 tablespoon white vinegar
¼ teaspoon dried savory
8 tomato slices, ¼ inch thick

Cook spinach as package directs, but drain very, very well. Press down with a fork in order to get all liquid possible out of it.

In medium bowl, combine the spinach and 3 table-spoons melted butter or margarine, the eggs, milk, onion, 1 ¼ teaspoons salt (or less), and ¼ teaspoon pepper, vinegar and savory. Generously butter 8 or 9 custard cups. Divide the spinach mixture evenly in the custard cups and place them in shallow roasting pan in 1 inch of hot water. Bake 35-40 minutes, or until custard sets. Remove from oven and take out of water. Custards may be wrapped in foil and placed on back of stove to keep warm until ready to serve, or may be placed in the oven, leaving the door open. Sprinkle the tomato slices with salt and pepper and invert cups, placing spinach custard on tomato slices. Serve on round platter.

All of the children at our house like this recipe . . .

BAKED ACORN SQUASH

Cut acorn squash in half and cook in water until tender. In oven set at 375°, bake squash for 15-20 minutes. Just before serving, add:
1 tablespoon butter
1 tablespoon brown sugar
2 tablespoons crushed pineapple

Agnes Loe is an Alpha Phi alumnae friend from early days in Salem. She and her husband, Chet, have lived in Albuquerque for some years. It's always a happy time when our paths cross. Here is her delightful contribution to the Vegetable Section.

BROCCOLI

2 packages chopped broccoli, thawed
¼ pound butter (reserving 2 tablespoons)
½ cup chopped onion

½ cup water
8 ounces processed cheese spread
3 well-beaten eggs
Bread crumbs

Saute onion in butter. Add ½ cup water. Stir until it comes to a boil. Add processed cheese spread, then add uncooked broccoli and well-beaten eggs. Stir and put in greased casserole. Add crumb topping, mixed with 2 tablespoons butter reserved from above, melted. Agnes sometimes adds almonds to crumb topping.

Bake 30 minutes at 325°.

Chris Sloper is one of the best gourmet cooks in our former hometown of Salem. Besides that, she and Val, her husband, are favorites, because Mark and I double-dated with them for dinner on our first date. Chris makes everything taste good; and, besides, she has boundless energy so she is always "cooking up a storm." Here is her recipe for broccoli.

BROCCOLI

4 cups cooked (just done) broccoli, or 3 packages
frozen broccoli (chopped)
1 can cream of mushroom soup
½ cup sour cream
1 jar (1 ounce) sliced pimiento
1 cup sliced celery
⅛ teaspoon pepper
1 teaspoon salt
½ cup grated cheese

Combine all ingredients, except grated cheese, for sauce. Pour over broccoli. Top with grated cheese and bake 20 minutes at 350°.

Mrs. Sam Haley, of Salem, whose husband is the Public Utilities Commissioner, submits this delicious recipe. Thanks, Jean — the children love cauliflower this way.

CAULIFLOWER

Head of cauliflower
1 can Cream of Chicken soup (undiluted)
1 can Cream of Celery soup (undiluted)
Dash of cooking sherry
Cheese

Cut cauliflower in chunks. Par boil until not quite tender. Place in greased casserole and pour undiluted soups and sherry over it. Cover and bake at 350° for about 20 minutes. Remove lid and sprinkle grated cheese over top. Continue baking until cheese is melted.

Marge Horton is a "praying buddy" in the Congressional Wives Prayer Group. Her faith is an inspiration — you'll like her corn pudding, too.

CORN PUDDING

1 can cream-style corn
2 ½ cups milk (scald in double boiler)
2 eggs

Blend these ingredients with ½ cup of scalded milk:
½ cup sugar
½ cup flour
1 teaspoon salt

4 tablespoons cream
½ teaspoon prepared mustard
Cracker crumbs

Scald milk. Add corn. Add sugar mixture. Cook about 15 minutes, until thick. Add beaten eggs, cream and mustard. Cook 5 minutes more. Pour into greased, shallow pan. Top with buttered cracker crumbs. Brown in 350° oven.

Tom O'Dwyer's sister, Mary Long, shared this family recipe with a little prodding from Tom. Thanks to both of them.

CONCANNON POTATOES

2 cups mashed potatoes (packaged or fresh mashed)
3 or 4 green onions (chopped)
2 cups finely cut cabbage
Salt and pepper to taste
Butter
Water
Parsley

Put green onions to cook in water (and milk and butter, if processed potato flakes are used). Cook potatoes with green onions, and when done mash well. Cook cabbage (shredded) in separate pan of salted water, till tender but crisp. Drain well. Fold into potatoes and top with a tablespoon or so of butter. Garnish with large sprig of parsley.

From Peggy St. Louis, one of the first ladies I met after coming to Washington, and who is a charming person and hostess, comes this recipe for . . .

CUCUMBER A LA PEGGY

Get large firm cucumbers (one for each person). Pare, cut in half lengthwise and remove all the seeds. Put in boiling salted water. Cook until done, but not too soft.

Make a rich cream sauce (using your favorite recipe). Put drained cucumbers in buttered baking dish. Pour cream sauce over the top. Sprinkle generously with paprika. Heat thoroughly in 300° oven until hot clear through. Serve immediately.

Anne Sporre is one of the caterers in Astoria, Oregon. She shared this very special recipe with me. Mrs. Harry Steinbeck, who was our hostess, predicted that I'd want it. How right. It's marvelous with salmon.

CUCUMBER DILLY SOUFFLE

3 eggs (separated)
1 cup milk
2 cups shredded cucumber (drained)
1 ½ teaspoons salt
1 teaspoon onion
1 teaspoon sugar
Dash of pepper
¼ teaspoon dill
Garlic
2 tablespoons flour
1 teaspoon baking powder

Beat egg whites until stiff — mix in 2 tablespoons flour and 1 teaspoon baking powder. Fold into cucumber mix. Grease bottom of pan and place pan in hot water. Bake in 325° oven for 1 hour.

Vivian Adams, one of the "workhorses" of the Republican Party in Oregon, gave me this Greek recipe some years back. Thanks, Vivian, not only for the recipe, but for all of your labors in the vineyard of politics.

DOMATES GEMISTES

12 tomatoes (large, firm)
1 cup rice
½ teaspoon rosemary
¼ cup parsley
1 cup water
1 pound ground veal
1 ¼ cups olive oil
¼ teaspoon pepper
2 teaspoons sugar
1 cup Parmesan cheese
4 onions, grated
2 teaspoons salt
¼ teaspoon oregano
¼ cup currants
¼ cup pine nuts

Cut tops of tomatoes and scoop out inside pulp (reserving pulp). In large skillet, simmer ground veal, onions with water to cover for 25 minutes. Add rice, 1 cup olive oil, seasonings, parsley. Mix, and simmer for 30 minutes. Add chopped tomato pulp, sugar, currants, and pine nuts. Spoon mixture into tomato shells; sprinkle with grated Parmesan cheese, place in large baking dish. Add 1 cup hot water, ¼ cup oil. Bake at 350° for 30 minutes. Serve hot or chilled.

Makes 12 stuffed tomatoes, but it usually takes 2 per person.

From my favorite "Blueberry lady" comes this recipe for parsnips. Thanks, Mrs. Phil Grenon.

EXTRA-SPECIAL PARSNIPS

12 medium parsnips, pared
1 cup crushed pineapple, undrained
½ cup orange juice
½ teaspoon salt
½ teaspoon shredded orange peel
2 tablespoons brown sugar
2 tablespoons butter

Cook parsnips, covered, in small amount of boiling salted water until tender, about 25-30 minutes. Drain. Split lengthwise and place in 10 x 6-inch baking dish. Combine pineapple with next 4 ingredients; pour over parsnips. Dot with butter. Bake in moderate oven (350°) for 30-35 minutes. Spoon sauce over several times during baking.

Another of Charlotte Wendel's recipes — I like the pine nuts!

GREEN PEAS CONTINENTAL

2 tablespoons butter
1 clove garlic, halved
1 teaspoon prepared mustard
1 teaspoon salt
¼ cup water
1 package (10 ounces) frozen peas
¼ cup pine nuts or almonds

Melt butter with garlic in medium sauce pan. Add mustard, salt, water and peas. Cook until tender, remove garlic. Place in serving dish and sprinkle nuts down the middle.

Lorna Belle Hammer, of Salem, says, "This looks pretty awful when you're mixing it, but it is really very good."

LORNA BELLE'S BROCCOLI SUPREME

1 package frozen broccoli (thaw slightly and chop)
2 cups cooked rice
1 jar (8 ounces) plain cheese spread (processed)
1 can Cream of Chicken soup (undiluted)
¾ cup potato chips or bread crumbs

Lightly mix all ingredients except chips or crumbs. Put in 1 ½-quart casserole and top with crushed potato chips or buttered bread crumbs. Bake at 350° for 30 minutes or until brown and bubbly.

Now here's a recipe from Mrs. Fred Hoefke of Salem (her husband used to collect your State Income Tax, if you are an Oregon resident), and Maxyne Davis, of Lake Oswego, tells us about a clever way to serve stuffed mushrooms.

MRS. HOEFKE'S STUFFED MUSHROOMS

Saute finely chopped stems of 20 mushrooms and 3 shallots, chopped, in 4 tablespoons butter. Add 2 cups soft bread crumbs, a dash of Worcestershire sauce, and salt and pepper to taste. Fill caps, place small square of bacon on each filled cap. Arrange in buttered baking dish, bake the mushrooms in a moderate oven (350°) for about 20 minutes. These can be made ahead of time.

MAXYNE DAVIS' METHOD OF SERVING STUFFED MUSHROOMS

Place each hot stuffed mushroom on a Chinese soup spoon (the porcelain 25-cent variety before inflation), all setting up on a tray. Adorn one corner of the tray with a flat bunch of Kale. Each mushroom is to be slipped into the mouth. "Emily wouldn't approve but select size accordingly. I use a footed tray and it is quite effective and fun. Have one of the children follow you with a smaller tray to pick up empty spoons."

The children planned a surprise birthday party for me last year. They invited close friends. We were all amused when they said to Peggy Stanton (wife of Congressman William Stanton of Ohio), "We have you down for peas." Peggy's Peas with Peanuts are great. But so is Peggy, who has perhaps the best sense of humor around the Hill!

PEGGY'S PEAS AND PEANUTS

1 teaspoon sugar
½ can (6-ounce) cocktail peanuts
1 package frozen peas
Salt to taste (if necessary)

Kathryn Lambert of Salem sent me this Spiced Carrot recipe on a card when she was resting in San Diego, California. It's nice to be remembered by your friends when they are traveling.

It does take all of the two hours to bake this.

Kathryn says this is an unusual way to do carrots and good to bake while you have a roast in.

SPICED CARROTS

3 cups sliced carrots
2 small onions
2 tablespoons butter
1 teaspoon salt
½ teaspoon pepper
⅛ teaspoon nutmeg
⅛ teaspoon cloves
1 teaspoon sugar
2 tablespoons flour
2 cups strained tomato juice
½ cup water

Fry onions in butter 5 minutes. Put in other ingredients. Pour into buttered covered casserole and bake 2 hours or until done.

Congressional junkets are always under scrutiny; but if they can produce recipes like this, why not! One of my friends from the House side of Congress recently brought this recipe back from the wife of our Ambassador to Uraguay — Caroline Adair.

STUFFED TOMATOES

Scoop out centers of 6 tomatos. Fill with:
2 cups bread crumbs, dipped in milk
1 teaspoon chopped parsley
1 chopped onion
2 whole eggs
½ cup of inside pulp of tomatoes
½ cup grated cheese
Season your favorite way

Mix ingredients, then fill in tomatoes. Sprinkle with grated cheese, top with small pieces of butter. Bake in moderate oven until filling is set and lightly browned.

*From Lakeview, Oregon, comes this tasty
recipe. A friend of Mrs. John McDonald's
prepared this for her when we were coming
to dinner during a campaign swing.*

STUFFED ZUCCHINI SQUASH

Parboil 12 zucchini squash. Boil whole, gently,
until barely tender. Drain and cool. Put on a board
and cut in half lengthwise. Scrape out insides of
squash and set aside. Invert squash shells on a towel
to dry completely.

Meanwhile, put ¼ cube of butter in a pan. Add ½ of
a medium-sized onion, *well* chopped, and 1 small
clove garlic, minced fine, and cook until golden.

Chop insides of squash. Squeeze water out. Add
chopped squash to onion and garlic. If there is not
enough filling, chop a whole, cooked squash and add.
Cook gently until moisture is absorbed. Remove from
heat. Add a big handful of parsley leaves (no stems)
finely chopped. Do not cook after parsley has been
added. Add to cooled mixture a *big* handfull (or
about ¾ cup) grated Romano or Parmigiano cheese.
Grate it yourself. Do not use that which comes grated
from the store. Add salt and pepper to taste. You may
want to add more grated cheese. Fill squash until
slightly rounded. Put a pat of butter on each squash
half, lay flat in a well-buttered pan and bake at
350° until golden brown, ½ to ¾ of an hour.

From Mildred Reed of my book club in Bethesda comes this recipe for Tomato Pudding. Mary Jane Lugibihl, of Pandora, Ohio, sent the same recipe, so you can see how far a good recipe will travel.

TOMATO PUDDING

2 cans (10-ounce) tomato Puree
½ cup boiling water
2 cups brown sugar
½ teaspoon salt
1 cup melted butter
12 slices bread with crusts removed, cut into squares

Add sugar, salt and boiling water to puree and boil for 5 minutes. Place bread squares in casserole; pour melted butter over bread. Add hot puree mixture and bake covered, 30 minutes, at 375°. Uncover and bake another 10 minutes.

This is a Walnut Zucchini recipe which the Forum Restaurant in New York City sent me. The fact that it uses a good Oregon product — walnuts — makes it appealing. The trick is to peel the zucchini.

WALNUT ZUCCHINI

2 zucchini squash, peeled and sliced
10 walnut halves
¼ pound butter
Salt and pepper to taste
Monosodium glutamate

Saute walnuts in hot butter until slightly browned. Add zucchini, flavor with salt, pepper and monosodium glutamate. Bring to a high heat and saute zucchini at high heat until browned and tender.

Makes 2 servings.

Nearly every tourist to Washington manages to get down to Williamsburg, Virginia, to sightsee that restored Colonial town. This recipe is courtesy of the Williamsburg Inn, a favorite of Colonial times and the present, as well.

WILLIAMSBURG INN BAKED CARROT LOAF

2 pounds medium-size tender carrots
3 eggs
3 ⅓ tablespoons sugar
2 teaspoons salt
1 ½ tablespoons melted butter, unsalted
1 ⅓ teaspoons cornstarch
13 tablespoons milk
13 tablespoons cream (20 percent)

Cover the carrots with water and cook until tender. Let cool slightly. Peel carrots and put through food chopper or sieve. Beat the eggs, yolks and whites separately, until light and add to the carrot mixture, together with the sugar, salt and melted butter. Mix cornstarch with a little milk to make a paste and add to the above mixture. Last, stir in the milk and cream and mix well. Place in a buttered baking dish and set in a pan of hot water to bake. Bake in 350° oven for 45 minutes or until light brown. Serve hot.

Makes 10 servings.

We're big on zucchini recipes in this section, but each one is enough different and will help use up the crop if you have a patch in your garden.

This recipe comes from Toni Carter, who is a sister Delta Kappa Gamma (National Honorary for active teachers).

ZUCCHINI A LA TONI CRATER

2 pounds zucchini
1 small onion, or several green ones
Small clove garlic
Parsley
½ cup dry bread crumbs, or 2 slices, cubed
2 eggs
1 tablespoon oil
½ cup grated cheese

Cut up zucchini, cook in salted water. Drain and add onion, garlic, parsley and bread. Beat eggs and add with oil and cheese. Dot with butter and bake at 325° for about 45 minutes.

A bit of oregano gives this dish an Italian flavor.

Another contribution from a campaign chairman. Little did I know, when I dated one of Irene Carey's sons in college, that she and her husband would be part of a very important campaign team.

ZUCCHINI CASSEROLE

Wash, slice thin (don't peel) and boil 3 pounds zucchini squash for 10-12 minutes (do not overcook). Set aside.

Combine:
3 beaten eggs
½ teaspoon garlic
½ teaspoon pepper
1 teaspoon salt
½ teaspoon monosodium glutamate

Fold this mixture into cooked squash. Place in a greased 10 x 10-inch pan. Cover with:
½ to ¾ cup cracker crumbs
Sharp grated cheddar cheese, to suit taste

Bake 30 minutes at 350°.

Index

Appetizers

Beverages

Breads & Jams

Cakes

Cookies

Desserts

Entrees

Entrees *(cont'd)*

Pickles

Pies

Rice & Other Starches

Salads & Salad Dressings

Seafood

Vegetables

AUG